MAKE AMERICA
SANE AGAIN

A Mental Health Experts Weighs In

MICHAEL ADAMSE, PH.D

Inspired Forever Books

Dallas, Texas

Make America Sane Again
A Mental Health Expert Weighs In

Inspired Forever Books
Dallas, Texas
(888) 403-2727
https://inspiredforeverbooks.com
"Words with Lasting Impact"

Library of Congress Control Number: 2022910314

Paperback ISBN 13: 978-1-948903-67-7

Printed in the United States of America

Disclaimer: The information in this book is intended to furnish users with general information on matters that they may find to be of interest. The content shared on these pages is not intended to replace or serve as substitute for any audit, advisory, or other professional advice, consultation, or service.

Dedication

This book is dedicated to you, the reader,
with the hope that you will embrace a positive attitude and experience
the good that continues to be found in America.

TABLE OF CONTENTS

ACKNOWLEDGMENTS

My favorite part of writing is this section of the book. Here I can express my gratitude to those who have supported my work. A huge thank-you to my amazing wife and best friend, Suzanne, who has always championed my literary efforts. Writing is often a solitary endeavor, and her continual input as my thought partner has been invaluable. Her insights and guidance help to bring my writing to a higher state of excellence.

My appreciation for my gifted editors Allison Janse and Bob Lan, whose expertise helped to make this book the best it could be.

Thanks to Allison Duine and her team at Intersection Online for crafting a great cover and website. Interpreting my concepts and bringing them to reality was a joy.

I have been blessed by my friends and family, who have encouraged and supported my writing throughout the years. A special thank-you goes out to my lifelong friend J. C. Smith, who has seen me through many challenges as well as many adventures. My heartfelt appreciation goes to Becky and Don Campagna, Christy and Larry Hierholzer, the

Kamenstein family (Carol, David, Tracy, and Sloan), Adriana Girolami, Evelyn Soto-Inglesias, Dr. Larry Kawa, and my daughters, Elise and Dana.

Finally, I want to thank my many clients over the years who have taught me the various aspects of the human condition.

INTRODUCTION

I was compelled to author this book. I could no longer sit by and watch America's mental health continue to deteriorate. My background in philosophy and clinical psychology prepared me to address America's current mental state from two important perspectives. When I told my friends and clients that I was planning to write a new book addressing what I viewed as the nation's urgent needs, they followed up by asking for the title I was considering. When I responded with "Make America Sane Again," they almost always politely smiled and said, "Good luck with that!" or, "How many volumes in that series?" Sadly, those reactions reinforced what I already knew. Pessimism has taken a deep hold on America.

As I write this, fear and distrust are running rampant in the individual and collective psyches. Becoming enmeshed in a conventional war, or worse, remains a possibility. Terrorism is firmly ensconced in America's collective mind. Horrific gun violence is commonplace, the populace is deeply divided over numerous political issues, and of course, our planet is edging even closer to being on life support.

Things have never been this bad, and the stakes are high. America has gone off the rails, and we are well on our way to collapse, right?

That's partially but not completely true from a psychological perspective. For certain, we are at a crossroads where our very way of thinking can shift in a direction that would be particularly challenging to alter. This is especially true of our younger generations, who are already missing an education that emphasizes critical analytic thinking skills. A strong case can be made that it's too late to change society's course. The good news is that it's not too late to alter *your* course.

Previous generations were encouraged to think through a challenge by using logic, intellectual discipline, and creative problem solving. A trustworthy source of information provided you with the raw material, and you processed it from there. Opposing views were to be respected and provided learning experiences. If you only seek out information that reinforces what you already believe, then you will inevitably have an incomplete picture.

If you find yourself confused about what is going on in America, that's a good sign. The conflicting messages you are exposed to are just that: confusing.

The phrase "Do your own research" is simply another way of saying, "Think for yourself."

We are in a bad place but not a hopeless one. What we will need to embrace is an approach that ultimately empowers us as individuals to think for ourselves. That sounds simple enough, but you'll see in the following pages that multiple factors are in constant competition to influence your thinking and behavior. I want you to be fully aware of those factors so that you are as free as possible to draw your own conclusions.

Let's first address an assumption in the title, which presumes that America was once sane and that we are not now. Of course, neither extreme view is wholly accurate. This country has been through rough times before and recovered, but I believe that we as a nation have been much saner than we are today.

The rates of addiction, suicide, depression, and anxiety disorders are at an all-time high. Many people are lonely and increasingly detached from meaningful human interaction. Most Americans fail to take care of themselves physically, psychologically, and spiritually.

As our starting point, it's important to be honest with ourselves if we're to move from despair to hope.

As a baby boomer, I grew up during a time when children learned about chores, the importance of faith, and doing our homework. We played outside in all types of weather and ate dinner as a family. Educators were respected, and if there were any problems at school, our parents sided with the teachers. One of my favorite memories occurred when our local police officer took me for a ride in his cruiser at the age of eight and turned on the siren and lights. It was a thrill. My love for aviation was met with trips to our local airport to peer into the windows of aircraft parked on the ramp before fences became the norm. Sadly, those days are over.

Of course, there were challenges as well. The threat of nuclear war was real, and air-raid drills were regularly practiced. Segregation was the rule of law in several states. There were other problems, but somehow a sense of optimism prevailed.

That is not the America we're in now. Instead, multiple nationally scaled challenges are driving Americans into record physical and psychological distress levels. I address those in turn.

Make America Sane Again aims to provide you with sound psychological insights and principles to help you understand on a deeper level what is happening. Much of what appears here applies to other nations, but our focus is on the United States.

Historically, the American people have always prided themselves on individualism and a deep-seated belief in fending for themselves. Yet when we are faced with an externally generated threat, Americans have a powerful ability to pull together to meet the challenge head-on. The attacks of September 11, 2001, offer a case in point.

On the other hand, our current domestic conflicts often are not managed through a philosophy that emphasizes tolerance and compromise. Issues generated politically and otherwise quickly devolve into polarized positions that can divide people more than any outside threat could dream of doing.

As you read through this book, keep in mind that your attitude, and the behavior that follows along with your beliefs, will determine your path forward. That path, in turn, solely depends on your ability to process information thoroughly. It requires motivation to carefully consider different points of view and come to your own conclusions. Doing so is a considerable challenge in a world that often tries to convince you that opinion is fact.

Accepting personal responsibility is the overarching theme of this book and a goal for all of us. Blaming others seems to be a national pastime, and I am hoping to help reverse that trend.

For many Americans, it comes down to a choice between succumbing to fear and a feeling of helplessness or deciding that our domestic challenges provide an opportunity to reflect on our own lives: what is truly most important and what we can do to change for the better.

I originally planned to write a book that explored the psychological lessons we can all learn from the pandemic. In reflecting carefully on its impact throughout the world, I then decided to go in another direction entirely. If we address the pandemic only in strictly medical and biological terms, we will have missed an important lesson that, if studied carefully, has the power to transform our individual and collective lives.

Having been on the front lines of the mental health tsunami that has impacted so many lives, directly and indirectly, I do not need any studies or statistics to drive home the message that this pandemic has caused massive psychological distress. It's evident to everyone.

However this all plays out, we need to go deeper. Many Americans have comorbid conditions that have made them much more vulnerable to COVID-19. Most of those underlying issues are within a person's behavioral control. We address this issue head-on.

We also discuss the double-edged sword of technology, addictions, and violence, as well as other concerns that undermine America's mental health.

Once we firmly identify what is going wrong, I proffer my advice on what you as an individual can do to help make America sane again. If you are blessed with a good measure of common sense, you'll find what I have to say already familiar to your way of thinking. Like I often tell people, "It isn't rocket science."

My hope is that you study the blueprint I am about to lay out for you and see for yourself that fear can be readily tamed through a mindset that embraces rational thinking, perspective taking, and optimism.

I think we should be aware and concerned about America's mental health, but not panicked. Panic subverts rational thinking and simplifies complex issues into a primitive state of fear—and if unchecked, fear leads to heightened anxiety and forms of learned helplessness–based depressive states.

If you tend to be an optimistic type of person, much of what you read will be refreshing. However, this is not a Pollyannaish view of a world where all our problems are solved by sitting around a campfire singing songs and holding hands. I live in the real world and know fully well that our individual and societal lives are fraught with real and draining struggles. This can undoubtedly be a challenging and even tragic life to live for so many. I spend fifty hours a week witnessing genuine pain and suffering of all types, so I get it.

If you are prone to a pessimistic orientation, I make the case for why it's in your best interest to work on changing that. It's good for you and the rest of us. Whatever your attitude, I appeal for you to be introspective: willing to reflect on your own issues and what might be preventing you from seeing the good in the world. It turns out that our worldview is a complex confluence of biological, cultural, and environmental factors. Rarely can we identify any single factor as to why we focus on the positive versus the negative potential.

The rise of pessimism leads us to the canary in the coal mine. In case you are not familiar with that phrase, up until very recently, coal miners would often bring a canary with them into the mines where they worked. The canaries, being more sensitive to the presence of carbon monoxide, would die or fall ill well before any human would. The birds served as an early-warning sign that gave the miners enough time to avoid imminent danger.

Think of this book in some ways as an early warning. I hope that you consider the chapters that follow as an invitation to view our national issues in some ways as a learning opportunity. Unless we get a collective grip on what is truly happening to us on a deeper psychological level, the shift away from individual and collective optimism is at risk. Yes, even optimistic individuals can be worn down over time. I consider myself a realistic optimist and not an alarmist. At the same time, we cannot afford to ignore the power of negative messaging as propaganda. In my view, the canary might be starting to gasp for air.

One more point: faith is a deeply personal matter. What you choose to believe is up to you. However, in my view, faith can serve as a secret weapon that, if embraced fully, cannot be shaken no matter what happens during our journey on this earth. I have experienced this repeatedly in my work, witnessing the power of faith to comfort people facing unimaginable tragedies. So now is the perfect time to reflect on your spiritual life. I have some thoughts about that in the concluding chapter.

Given the book's title and its echoing of a phrase that's now in the popular zeitgeist, I'd recommend you not spend any mental energy trying to figure out what "side" I might be on, nor should it matter. The pages to come apply to everyone and are based on sound psychological principles. My intent is to see what we can do to heal America, not add to the problem by creating any more discord by being misperceived. I cannot control how you will receive my writing, but I'm entirely in control of my intent, which is to have you more fully understand what is happening to us as a nation.

The first part of the book addresses serious issues facing us that profoundly affect our mental health. The latter part suggests some ways that you can individually improve your own well-being. That, in turn, helps everyone.

Many of my suggestions and insights might appear simplistic. That is intentional. I want you to move through much of the fog that clouds our way toward living a fuller and more meaningful life where a return to a saner America is possible. The path forward is clear if we intelligently learn to manage the influences that work to distract us.

This quote from Gandhi has been quite meaningful for me:

> If we could change ourselves, the tendencies in the world would also change. As a man changes his own nature, so does the attitude of the world change toward him. We need not wait to see what others do.

Remember that, very often, the simplest of truths are the most profound.

Let's get started.

EXPERT WITNESS

My life has been blessed. I have spent over ninety thousand hours working with clients who have experienced every kind of stress you can think of—and many, I promise you, you couldn't imagine. I witness enough human drama to fill a season of reality TV easily in a single day, but my stories are not the work of fiction. They reflect the many difficulties of life that range from manageable issues to tragic. I have a great deal of affection for my clients; they are good people going through a tough time.

I have been truly fortunate that I've never personally experienced a pessimistic view of humanity in all this exposure to stress. In fact, my understanding of the human condition has deepened such that I have found quite true the statement that we're more alike than not. No one is exempt from life's challenges. While every life journey is unique, there are times when an event or series of events creates a common context in which we all find ourselves.

Americans are going through such a time. We have our collective hands full, between the pandemic, political division, and other far-reaching issues.

My professional training has taught me to identify and treat a wide range of psychological problems. Included in that education was a requirement that we as students undergo our own course of intensive psychotherapy. I easily embraced that, as in my early twenties I had more than a few issues to explore. I have gone back into psychotherapy a few times since, during some personal life challenges. In my profession, it's essential to experience "the other side of the couch," especially so that you become aware of your issues and not project them onto the therapeutic relationship. Psychotherapy is a very complex process but provides the practitioner with essential tools to be successful in helping others.

I learned something early on in my career, and it's helped me through to this day. It is an obvious but difficult lesson for me, especially at first, as I have a strong drive to problem solve. While most issues can be addressed by teaching better coping skills and providing well-timed insights, not everything is fixable.

I cannot bring back a loved one who has taken their own life and leaves family and friends with gut-wrenching pain that is often mired in guilt. I am usually unable to comfort a spouse who lost their partner after sixty-plus years of marriage. I cannot get someone to stop excessive behaviors without their commitment. Psychotic delusions are difficult to challenge through reason. The list goes on.

Yet there are great successes. I see changes each day that underscore that people can often move beyond their challenges and find new ways of experiencing a fuller life. At the very least, I can offer an empathic ear, which is a major therapeutic tool. Always remember that listening is different than hearing. Genuine listening means a careful expenditure of energy in the service of someone who has a story to tell. One need not be a therapist to be an empathic listener.

Consider this example of compassionate listening. Many instances are embedded in my memory after having witnessed several thousand personal stories over my professional life. One in particular concerns a World War II veteran who asked me to tell it so that others might learn from it.

While serving in the Army Reserve Medical Command part of my duty involved assessing veterans who had suffered from posttraumatic stress disorder (PTSD). I was assigned to an outpatient clinic at a Department of Veterans Affairs hospital. Before interviewing each veteran, it was standard procedure to read their military personnel file to become familiar with the person's background. Each record contained the entire history of the veteran's service and was kept in a plain brown file that any military person would recognize.

As my interview was with a veteran who was, by this time, in his late seventies, I wasn't sure he'd remember the events in question clearly enough. I opened the file carefully as I needed to treat his case with his deserved due respect. Everything was documented in its original typewritten form. It felt as though I was holding a sacred piece of history in my hands. It turns out I was. I had no idea what he had been through but would soon find out. I reviewed the usual information regarding training, unit assignments, and performance. I finally got to what the military refers to as an "after-action report." It's a document that can review any number of events, but in his case, I focused on his unit's battle with a German regiment in Italy in 1944.

It described the battle's events in detail, which was a high-tempo engagement with fierce hand-to-hand combat. I could not imagine what it was like to kill a stranger fighting for their country. In some other time and place, they could have been friends. I did not know what to expect when I greeted the veteran and took him into my office.

"Humbled" would be a good word to describe my experience for the next hour. I quickly established a rapport and asked this veteran to tell me his story in any way he wanted. Though there is a structure to diagnostic interviewing, I knew that if I allowed the conversation to flow organically, I would get what I needed.

He started by sharing some information about himself, and I listened carefully for the transition as to why he was there to see me. I knew it was coming. It always did. At one point, he began to talk about his military service and then, suddenly and abruptly, he broke down into tears and started choking on his words. It was a radical emotional breakdown in less than a few seconds. I asked him to just take his time. He gathered his composure and began to tell me that after all these years, he could not get the face of the German he killed out of his mind. It was the face of a young man filled with terror.

He had survived a fatal and traumatic hand-to-hand combat situation without physical injury, but the emotional scars had continued throughout his life. The killing was related in great detail, and the horror was not something that had been buried all these years. Instead, he had kept his suffering to himself, lived a long and productive life, and felt a need to cleanse himself with someone. He went on to tell me about all the deaths of his friends and his guilt for surviving the war. He never spoke to anyone in his family about his combat experiences. Let us remember that he served at a time when veterans weren't as readily identified as suffering from military-related psychological trauma as today.

For my part, I could say nothing that would comfort him other than genuinely communicating empathy and thanking him for his service and sharing his story with me. It turns out that giving him the proper time and space to tell it was more than okay. The fact that he could open up in a trusting environment without judgment was therapeutic. At the end of the interview, he firmly shook my hand and let me know that sharing his story with someone else after all these years was a relief. He also asked me to tell anyone I wanted to about his traumatic event and that he wished people would genuinely appreciate what war veterans on all sides went through. I felt honored that he felt comfortable enough to share his experience and suggested he participate in a combat veterans' support group.

So what does this story have to do with a lesson learned? Everything. This is an example of gratitude and a reminder of what other generations have done to protect and build our country. One can easily forget what sacrifices were made on our behalf. An appreciation of our history, the good and the troubled times, is all part of our collective American experience.

While it's not realistic to experience each human encounter in depth, it's beneficial to remember that each person who crosses our paths has a richly textured and unique backstory. Most people who passed by the veteran whose story I shared probably overlooked him. I try to view every client as a living novel, an extraordinarily complex blend of factors that makes each of us unique.

Witnessing *any* story strengthens our bonds. When these bonds are reinforced over time, they create a psychological glue that keeps us intimately connected so that, collectively, we can withstand any challenge better. It really works that way. In a sense, it's about building psychological reserves through interconnectedness that we can fall back on when a challenge arrives—and as any student of history knows, major challenges are inevitable.

Too often we see a crisis pull people together only temporarily. Once things return to normal, many go back to following their individual paths. Early intentions to stay in touch, while well-meaning, are often lost in modern distractions. That is not true around the world, of course. Societies that place a high value on social connectedness are far better prepared, especially those that emphasize intergenerational bonds.

The flip side to witnessing others, of course, is having them witness you. We all have our challenges, and sharing with others is a critical component of psychological well-being. Physical proximity promotes interaction, and social distancing is antithetical to human nature. In times of fear and collective threat, we are programmed to pull together, as there truly is comfort and strength in numbers.

Then there's loneliness, the silent killer. I see it in my practice every day. All psychological problems are magnified when an individual feels alone or, even worse, abandoned. COVID is an extreme example of the negative impact of social isolation. Children and adolescents need social skills training and experiences that are critical to human development. Additionally, we index much of our behavior and attitudes based on peers and role models. It's important to be realistic about internet-based teaching; it fails miserably in comparison to in-class instruction—in children especially. Much of what we learn from others is nuanced, and that is lost online. We take a closer look at this issue later.

Older individuals who live alone are also highly vulnerable to the effects of less human contact. Unfortunately, advancing age is not something that garners the respect that it deserves. America could learn better by paying attention to other cultures that honor elders.

At the same time, to those who have access to technology, the ability to reach out is limited only by effort. Nothing will ever entirely supplant the need for actual face-to-face interaction. Still, the world is connected and interconnected in a way that allows us to reach across streets and continents in real time: an obvious opportunity.

Many of my clients have established friendships with people all over the world through various social media platforms. Some have been intentional and others random cyberencounters. Whatever the original connection, bonds have been formed that cross all traditional socioeconomic barriers. In my view, this is an exciting chance to make our world a better place by understanding others in the next state or around the globe.

You do not need to be an expert to be a witness, but you do have to be willing to listen. A witness who tries their utmost not to insert their own biases is the best kind. Advice is fine, but the key ingredient to connecting with others is that they should feel understood.

In all my work over the years, I've seen this theme repeatedly. Remember this simple equation: frustration leads to aggression turned either inward or outward. Frustration is disarmed through understanding. Understanding does not mean accepting everything you come across. That's not realistic, and many things are unacceptable. Tapping into your common sense usually guides the way.

By the end of this book, I hope that you thoroughly understand the critically important part you play in moving this nation forward in a positive direction. The situation is not hopeless, and you are not helpless. Americans have traditionally never viewed themselves as victims.

My point is simply this: you, the reader, are the most important piece of the puzzle in how to make America sane again.

STOP FEEDING
THE ELEPHANT

We are going to deal with this head-on. There is an elephant in the room, and it's not small either. In fact, it's so huge it's sucking up all the air. In all its forms, the media—that elephant—has the power to be the dead-center engine that drives fear and anxiety in a psychological environment where we are programmed to pay close attention to anything that appears as a threat. The time line works like this: fear-based conflict creates drama, and drama creates interest. That tried-and-true formula is essential to understanding this concept in order to evaluate and separate what seems to be fact from what I like to refer to as "enhanced reality."

Enhanced reality refers to any spin that is placed on a factual news story. Even facts are subject to careful editing that can change the entire trajectory of a report. Contemporary media outlets are dominated by carefully designed programming. The increasing tailoring of online information to fit your own individual interests leads to increasingly targeted news reported in a manner that matches your beliefs.

A quick statement to start: the free functioning of news outlets is necessary in any society that values open communication. Democratic societies depend on the unrestricted dissemination of news and opinion. Bringing accurate information to the public is the core feature of responsible journalism. Indeed, many fine journalists and news agencies worldwide rightfully pride themselves on being sources of unbiased and responsible reporting. In reality, though, a shift of seismic proportions has taken place right under our proverbial noses.

That shift is from print newspaper and twice-per-day television news broadcasting to a twenty-four-hour news cycle delivered through cable or internet sources. Nonstop purely news-based reporting is a nonsustainable business model for holding onto viewers. Something else is needed. It requires continual content to feed viewers, and to do that, media outlets have two powerful strategies that can keep consumers engaged: fear and opinion.

Fear is generated through the anticipation of negative events. Therefore, if news organizations can mobilize fear by emphasizing how terrible things are and how they might be even worse in the future, such media are more likely to keep you engaged. If they throw in a positive story here and there, it creates a yo-yo effect where emotions are subject to manipulation.

While potentially informative and interesting, opinion pieces are also a source of *propaganda*, the deliberate manipulation of information to further a cause or belief while conveniently leaving out alternative points of view.

Negative energy begins to fuel itself when polarized positions become increasingly solidified, and intolerance of opposing views is the new norm.

When media outlets hammer away at fear and negativity, over time those emotions simply bypass our conscious thinking and make a nice new home in our unconscious minds, which, many would argue, represent the playground of our true motivations, drives, and attitudes. Without even realizing it, our attitudes are displayed in our behaviors toward others. In this upside-down world, the conservative and the liberal both become increasingly intolerant, and we all know where that leads.

News dissemination has morphed during the last four decades from a slow-moving transfer of information that was primarily fact-based to heavily skewed opinion and commentary. While interesting and even sometimes insightful, commentary can also take the work out of coming to our own conclusions. We can quickly arrive at a worldview that is prepackaged and hopelessly unbalanced. Let us move this line of thinking a bit further.

Our complex matrix of experiences, personality, intelligence, and attitudes alters what we claim is then an objective opinion.

There's also the issue of dumbing down, which is remarkably simple to accomplish. All that needs to happen is to overload an individual with endless "facts," opinions, and predominantly negative messaging. That combination can lead to forming a simplistic view of complex issues to help us cope in the service of reducing potential confusion. If the media can add an element of personal dislike for someone in the news, that seals the deal in our unconscious.

Remember the truism I mentioned earlier that conflict creates drama and drama creates interest. Novels, films, and real-life events all take advantage of that formula, which works well when applied to benign entertainment. In real life, it's highly destructive to individuals and societies when the fear results in many psychological disorders, most notably anxiety and depression. *Anxiety* is the anticipation of a perceived upcoming negative event. *Depression* can be related to a mental state of learned helplessness where individuals believe that they can do nothing to influence their state of being.

Unbalanced, fear-based messaging elevates an individual's alert mode to one in which more negative information degrades psychological adaptability. We are, of course, programmed to pay close attention to potentially harmful stimuli. Repetitive negative stimuli create damaging stress.

Be mindful of the seduction that the news is simply there to inform you. Of course, it serves a powerful role in disseminating information, but the news is also there to serve itself. Namely, news functions as a business that depends on consumers in the form of viewers, listeners, and readers. Our most important defense is being smart consumers. I deliberately used the word "defense" because consumers are under attack.

Relentlessly exposed to stressful communications that are highly targeted to build fear, we are limited in our ability to cope with all this negativity. We can and inevitably do reach a point of psychological exhaustion that results in fatigue, anxiety, depression, and most important, reduced stress tolerance. I have seen it scores of times in my practice.

You will rarely hear about a certain hidden fact because no one mentions it very much and it is impossible to quantify:

Excessive stress degrades the immune system and sets the stage for self-destructive behaviors.

The mind and the human body are, of course, intricately connected. How you think has a significant impact on how you feel. Conversely, how you feel physically affects your mood and thought processing. You simply do not think as clearly when your mind and body are not in sync.

Any source of stress can contribute to a degradation of the immune system, and the pandemic has been a stressor of literally worldwide proportions. Fear has piggybacked on the virus with such force that any attempt to quantify the immediate and far-reaching, complex effects escapes metrics.

Media outlets that have a hidden agenda also have a major flaw. By "hidden agenda," I am referring to either an intentional or preconscious intent to magnify fear and discord. The flaw is an inherent failure to recognize that not all egos are created equally. We return to that point in a moment.

Unbalanced media messages use propaganda to win you over. Propaganda, as mentioned earlier, is the deliberate messaging of information that is biased or misleading. The use of carefully edited sound bites that provide an incomplete picture of what is taking place can lead a consumer to a misleading conclusion.

As an oversimplification, the ego is the mediator between our basic primitive drives (the id) and what we morally find acceptable or unacceptable (the superego). Most importantly, the ego has a critically important function in protecting us through *reality testing*, which refers to the ability to see situations for how they are instead of what we either hope or fear they might be. If your reality testing functions normally, your ability to place inputs from the outside world into perspective helps you assess information more rationally. A breakdown in this ability can cause or exacerbate both physical and psychological problems.

Keep in mind that fear trumps reason. Fear and reason have an inverse relationship. The more fearful we are, the less we can control our responses to whatever stressors we're facing. Consider phobias, for example. *Phobias* are a class of anxiety disorders that reflect excessive fear in the presence of a perceived dangerous stimulus. Phobic individuals almost always acknowledge that their fears are excessive and irrational, but that intellectual awareness isn't enough to calm them down.

Anticipatory anxiety, which is worry in advance of a perceived stressful event, compounds the problem. Awareness of danger can quickly escalate to a phobic state of mind if the messages are strong enough and repeated. If visuals can accompany the message, it will be even more effective.

I take a quick look at the stock market every day and am always amused by the choice of language that accompanies a tiny drop in value. Words like the market is "falling," "dropping," "panicking," and "sliding" are invariably accompanied by a picture of someone on the stock exchange floor who has an expression of obvious alarm and distress. On the other hand, if there's positive movement on the exchange, traders are shown looking excited and joyous.

All of this may seem innocent enough, except that it isn't. Text and imagery powerfully convey information that is often emotionally laden.

What if someone is particularly vulnerable to negative messaging? This has especially been the case with the pandemic. I know of a twenty-eight-year-old man who took his own life because he was afraid that he would get the virus. You read that correctly. He did not have the virus; he was fearful of getting it. He watched the news all day, and fear had overwhelmed him. In short, his reality testing was severely impaired.

Individuals with serious mental illness are especially at risk of having difficulty filtering through negative messaging. Care and consideration of how information is communicated should be any news organization's gold standard. Hype and sensationalism only create unnecessary anxiety.

One might ask the question as to whether the media can generate hope and optimism during uncertain times. Of course they can, but positive messaging isn't valued in a climate of negativity nor has it proved as profitable.

A balanced approach would go a long way in mitigating the trap to which polarization leads. Polarization is a self-defeating mental state as it fails to recognize the complexity of issues we are coping with as a nation.

Keeping news stories in proper perspective would help a great deal. So would creating a forum for a conversation between opposing positions. The key word here is "conversation" as opposed to "debate." A dialogue is not offensive or defensive. It is a listening-based exercise in rational discussion.

In a debate, unfortunately, the emphasis is on talking points that serve to push an agenda forward without properly acknowledging that another view has validity.

This is apparent during political debates where there is rarely a nod to the other person's point of view. I believe that candidates who agreed with something, *anything*, that the other person said would find their credibility increased.

Let us keep in mind that an index of intelligence is the ability to thoroughly understand at least two sides of the same issue simultaneously.

Violence and abuse of any kind are intolerable in any civilized society. Common sense dictates that many issues are not up for discussion or debate.

Time for a personal anecdote. My parents lived in Nazi-occupied Holland during the entirety of World War II. They shared stories of how all the lights in their village had to be turned off in the evenings so as to not provide Allied bombers with a path to Germany. They also spoke of the lack of food, persecution of the Jews and other targeted individuals, and a curfew that was strictly enforced each evening under penalty of death. The curfew's seriousness was emphasized when a violator's dead body was left in the street as a warning.

My father—I write this proudly—was a member of the underground that hid Jews and downed aircrew members until they could be transferred through a sophisticated system to the coast of Holland and on to England. On one occasion, my father was caught by a German patrol and had a gun put to his head. He talked his way out of it, as he spoke fluent German.

I share this story because my father was the most optimistic, positive person I have ever known. He never complained or spoke badly of anyone. He watched the news but knew that the world was a beautiful place to live. He was also a man of faith, and I know that was the source of his personal power.

Most importantly, our parents taught my siblings and I the importance of tolerance and to avoid generalizing, as every individual is unique.

For our nation today, if something extraordinary occurs, especially something tragic, we might be quick to say that people are terrible and that society is falling apart. Outliers always receive center stage; the more outrageous, the more attention they get. This attention to anomalies is a core problem. The truth is that events always occur that are out of the norm, and as the population increases and life becomes more complex, the possibility of unacceptable behaviors increases. Crowding especially increases stress, as several robust studies affirm.

My recommendation is to stop feeding the elephant by seriously reducing your exposure to the news. As you know, much of it is repetitive and will not help you reduce your worries. If you are an anxious person to begin with, it does not make sense to amplify that fear.

My own approach is simple. I watch a few headlines in the morning to get an idea of what is going on and move on with my day. I am on a news diet and doing much better since I started. I have lost ten ounces of negative brain activity already.

What and how much you watch is up to you, but be mindful of what excessive news exposure is doing to your worldview.

Repeated exposure to negative inputs can find a lovely home in your unconscious mind and ultimately influence how you see other people and how you act toward them. Be careful.

GETTING OFF
THE BLAME TRAIN

If we are ever going to make any serious progress, then we as a nation and individually need to work on our insatiable search for who or what to blame. Pointing fingers at institutions or individuals is a psychological trap if it becomes the dominant method of addressing problems.

Certainly, though, in some cases the responsibility for an issue lies squarely with someone or something. For example, we do not need to look very far to see that acts of violence clearly lie with the perpetrator and with underlying contributing factors that provide fertile soil for such tragedies. We deal with violence and frustration in a later chapter.

Blatant neglect and abuse of any kind should be identified, dealt with, and rectified. The list of issues worthy of blame is a long one. Once again, common sense should guide us in helping to determine who or what is blameworthy.

Identifying the source of an issue is a major step in assigning responsibility and hopefully finding ways to prevent things from happening again.

For now, let us take a closer look at why excessively ascribing blame can be a problem. If we are preoccupied with trying to assign blame, we risk not moving forward by searching for solutions.

Another factor to consider is the source that is claiming your attention and trying to influence you. That could be an individual or an entity like the media. So, yes, I am back to the media precisely because it has such a powerful influence on people's attitudes and behaviors.

I sometimes include a person's significant other in my work with clients in the therapy process. If couples or family therapy is warranted, my intervention strategies are tailored to meet the needs my clients and I mutually identify.

If I first meet with someone *before* I have met anyone else, such as a spouse, things can get interesting. This happens when I'm not clear from the initial contact that our sessions might eventually include other people. I might very well get a description of the other person or persons that could leave a negative impression to the untrained observer. And another truism: every story has two sides, at least. One could form a quite biased image based solely on what a client said.

Then, on more than a few occasions, upon meeting the other person or persons, the initial construction of the relationship my mind had as a working model is entirely upended. At other times, that construct is affirmed. In cases like that, someone else's behavior is clearly the causal agent. Addictions are a robust example of self-destructive behaviors that can and very often do destroy families.

Keep in mind that everyone has an agenda, something in their mind that seeks support or approval. Of course, that's neither good nor bad, but we need to be aware that the psychological marketplace buys and sells ideas all the time. If I want to sell you on an idea, I do my best to convince you of why my way of thinking is better for you. Nothing is wrong with that, as long as I always do a soft sell by respecting your thoughts and opinions.

My point is that whatever your source of information—even me—be vigilant because it is quite easy to form an opinion based on limited input. Moreover, that opinion can easily reinforce what you already believe. If the messaging is antithetical to what you hold onto, your mind may reject the message outright by dismissing it or the messenger. An intelligent approach to sizing up any meaningful and impactful issue is to try as much as possible to find out all the different sides of a story. That takes an investment in time and energy.

Key here is that what is important to you is very personal. Many issues that cross your life path can be dispatched quickly. Your time is often limited in our crazy-paced country, so you need to be selective about what you decide is most important in your life.

Also remember that people are not perfect by any means. Being overly critical of others is a slippery slope. Judging anyone without truly knowing in some depth who they are or what their situation is often leads to an incomplete picture.

During our 2020 presidential elections, I witnessed how deeply the blame game went and how polarized people were. I had new clients vetting me as to who I might be supporting so they could decide whether to work with me as a psychotherapist. As any well-trained mental health professional can attest, political inclinations do not have a place in the therapeutic relationship.

I was surprised at the intensity of anger and polarization and how much the political climate was affecting people's well-being. Individuals would say to me frequently that they hated this or that person.

Being hateful is such an extreme mental state that it depletes the psychological energy of those who entertain such powerful emotions. If you cannot find the good in someone, you're better off being indifferent to them.

With more than 338 million Americans in our country, there are many shades of gray. No two humans see or experience the world in the same way.

If America is to regain more of its sanity, it needs to become more forgiving and less judgmental. Overemphasizing the desire to blame just keeps us from moving forward.

One last point I'd like you to understand about the blame game deals with projection. The psychological process of *projection*, in very simple terms, is the mental process by which we attribute to others what is actually in our own minds. Projection colors many of our human interchanges and is typically below our level of awareness. An example might be that I am angry and frustrated and assume that another person is hostile when in fact, they're not. I may even provoke anger in them, which in turn reinforces what was my initial faulty impression.

If we identify a problem in ourselves for which we do not want to accept responsibility, we can project it onto someone else. This mostly unconscious process makes it easy to reject ownership of something inside ourselves that causes us discomfort.

Self-awareness through introspection is the key variable in play here if you want to understand yourself and others more fully.

If we can move past the blame game, we can find a path forward to accept personal responsibility. It's a very powerful and liberating orientation to life—and one desperately needed in these times.

TECHNOLOGY: THE TWO-EDGED SWORD

Technology has permeated all our lives to such a dramatic degree that describing its effect on us psychologically is far beyond the scope of this chapter. So, for now, consider how much it has become a part of your individual life. It is truly astounding.

Doubtlessly, technology has made many things much easier and improved and saved lives. Medicine, communication, transportation, and other fields have experienced quantum leaps in development. Many positive and exciting breakthroughs have elevated the quality of life. But as with all change, something is left behind when something moves forward.

All these changes have come at a price. America—indeed, the entire world—has often been affected in a not-so-good way.

Start with education. While one can argue that technology has made it far easier to access learning, certain problems arise.

Permit me an indulgence here. As I wrote earlier, I grew up in the baby boomer generation, far before computers and the kind of technology we see in place today. Along with my fellow students, we attended classes and studied. Papers required research that sometimes involved frequent trips to the library, which meant poring through card catalogs and staring at stacks of bookshelves, hoping to find a desired source. In short, we paid our dues. It helped promote self-discipline and self-esteem when we did well and a desire to do better next time if we didn't.

Having information immediately available at the click of a mouse beats going to the library in a snowstorm, but the trade-off comes with a cost. The development of certain values is lost online.

I learned a great deal during my schooling about nonacademic matters, such as goal setting and, just as important, the concept of deferred gratification. *Deferred gratification* involves putting off rewards by working hard now for a goal that may be far in the future.

I was blessed with the opportunity for a good education and my family's value system, which emphasized challenging work to achieve rewards. Self-sufficiency was a central theme in my upbringing. I worked full-time and went to get my education full-time. That solid foundation has helped me throughout my life, and I am grateful for it.

Back to current events, online education very often presents a watered-down learning process. This is not true in all cases, as some individuals can learn very efficiently online, depending on the course, its delivery, and the student's steadfast dedication to learning.

I have witnessed this evolution in learning directly, having been an adjunct professor at two universities over a period of fifteen years. I saw classes evolve from entirely classroom-based to a hybrid model that includes both in person and online instruction, to entirely online learning. Believing in a traditional teaching model, I elected not to teach any courses online as I thought the quality of the experience for the students and me would be degraded.

I had a glimpse of what the future held during one class I was teaching. My approach to teaching included walking around the classroom, and many students had their laptops open. I walked past a student who was too busy watching a sports event to notice my presence. He was a bit startled when I asked him how the game was going. I purposely did not wait for his response, hoping he would take a quick lesson from that interchange. Realistically, I surmised he would end up being more vigilant in the future.

Our recent experience with the pandemic resulted in the decision for most schools on every grade and age level to pivot from in-class teaching to online. Unfortunately, it was a lost period for many, especially for children.

My daughter Elise is a second-grade inner-city teacher of whom I am very proud. I asked her to describe what it was like to teach twenty-five seven-year-olds who were all online in their respective homes. "Dad, try keeping twenty-five children engaged in a remote learning environment while they're home. That's hard enough in the classroom."

I did not need to imagine any further.

"They are distracted and often live in single parent homes with siblings. The adults may or may not have an interest in their education. When the students finally did return to the classroom, much of my time was spent reminding them to keep their masks on."

The formative educational years are particularly important in creating the foundation for mental health. That happens through attaining successful proficiency in basic life skills. Those skills include self-control, perspective taking, communication, critical thinking, creativity, and making connections, to name a few. Making sure America is as healthy a place to grow up as possible starts at the earliest ages, which necessarily involves the education process.

So what is the major problem with online learning? The format makes it far easier to cheat, and the quality of the learning experience is compromised—not in all cases, but enough to make it a problem.

Here's where things get dicey. I know of someone who, after a serious accident, was required to take a driving course with the option of doing so online. He proudly told me he passed because his wife took it for him. Unfortunately, this happens all the time.

What if you are a nursing student taking a difficult course online—say, molecular biology? You know someone who is a whiz at it. The course may get outsourced, and the original student does not learn properly. Yes, safeguards such as testing centers and cameras monitoring the test-takers exist, but not always.

One would hope that such ethical violations are rare, but we need to be honest: cheating isn't an unusual practice. It never was, but online education makes it easier now more than ever.

A fair question now might be, "How does this affect America's psychological well-being?" If taking shortcuts to get a proper education becomes acceptable, and even worse, if cheating is okay to get ahead, we have created an ultimately self-defeating mindset. But how so?

When I described the importance of critical analytic thinking skills earlier, consider the fact that the student who downloads a paper from a site that provides this service does not enhance those skills. Instead, the student is relying on someone else to think for them—and probably without truly knowing or knowing how to vet the source of the information.

Another problem comes when an educator can't see or hear the students being taught. A great deal of the educational experience is missing when people aren't in the classroom benefitting from the social and intellectual situations the classroom provides.

I once busted a student whose paper was clearly beyond their intellectual level by finding the exact paper published online. I was a bit disappointed that the student did not bother to try and fool me more convincingly. When I failed the student, an administrator politely called and asked me to please adjust the grade upward so the student would pass. That is a whole other story.

There you have it. I am not an enthusiastic fan of online education. At the same time, I can appreciate it has its place in certain instances.

I was thinking about addressing this next issue in the chapter on addictions, but it's better off being tackled here: online gaming is a potentially serious addiction, not just entertainment.

In moderation, nothing is inherently wrong with *most* online gaming, as with many potentially addictive behaviors and substances. The problem is that online gaming is not something done in moderation among children, adolescents, young adults, and even some adults. The brain's reward centers are too activated to keep it in check.

I routinely survey my younger clients or their parents and find that individuals play online games thirty to fifty hours a week. Yes, you read that right. Think of it as the equivalent of a full-time job with overtime with nothing to show but a high score or a bested (or not) anonymous competitor. I am all for having fun but not at the expense of time that should be devoted to learning and studying. I see this problem all the time in my practice.

The opportunity to play at anything is a beneficial activity that helps us achieve a balanced life. In the world of video games, however, I have repeatedly seen that engaging in these games excessively can add to an individual's stress instead of mitigating it. Helping to make America sane again would be to recognize that short-term strategies for stress reduction create long term problems of their own.

I find it interesting that much of online gaming, anime, and other technologically based entertainment forms do not encourage the player to engage in co-creation. The imaginative part is programmed into most games, though, in fairness, some do encourage individual expression.

Gaming whose content is violent—and, even worse, explicitly violent—is a proven problem regarding mental health. Studies done years ago indicated that individuals exposed to aggressive peers or role models were much more inclined to be aggressive themselves. Unfortunately, research on the effect of violent video games indicates desensitization to the pain and suffering of others, a decline in empathy, and a commensurate proclivity to aggression.

It should not be surprising that the uptick in violence in young adults is related to violent media exposure.

Let us come back to the effects of decreased empathy. I know of a young girl who shared a picture of a duck that had died in her backyard. Her comment was, "I wish I had killed it because it was annoying me with all the noise it was making." Really? She came from a stable family, raised with good values but watched excessively violent anime. Anime is a wildly popular Japanese hand drawn and computer-generated themed animation. While much less common with females, we can see that aggressive inclinations can cross genders. Cyberbullying finds its roots in the ease of expressing aggression online and adolescent females are more likely to be the targets of attacks by other females.

A failure to experience empathy is a byproduct of violent gaming due to a reductionism where individuals are viewed as labels, objects, and obstacles in the way of the games' goal. It's only a game, right?

One last point about online addictions: obesity, poor eating habits, and a lack of physical exercise go hand in hand with excessive computer time.

I am a realist, so I know we can't put the genie back in the bottle. The pros and cons of technology are here to stay. The best we can hope for is that parents teach their children to create balance in their lives. Like everything else influencing a child's development, there is a window that passes, and whatever influence parents have will fade as the family ages, and peers supplant adults. It has always been that way.

Moving on to online social connectivity, here is where the two-edged sword comes into play. Social connectedness can certainly be enhanced through online connections. Support and information-sharing groups addressing every conceivable life issue are valuable sources, providing what the sources share is accurate. Witnessing other people's stories is especially important to those stressed or suffering. As we learned at the beginning of this book, the simple act of caring is a powerful expression of kindness that enhances well-being for both parties.

While technology is neither summarily good nor bad, it is powerfully seductive. The crucial factor is ultimately how you, the consumer, decide to interact with technology and how much (and how) it affects your well-being.

ANOTHER CLIMATE CHANGE

Another type of climate change has been having a profound effect on how most of us live our lives. It has nothing to do with global warming. I'm referring to what I call "social climate change."

What I am addressing specifically is the slow, almost imperceptible erosion of the depth of interactions that are required to establish and engage in quality human relationships.

A good starting point to help understand this erosion is the world of internet dating. A colleague of mine, Dr. Sheree Motta, and I authored a book in 1996 in the earliest stage of internet socialization and online dating. We were beginning to see clients who had become romantically involved with people they met online. There were no dating services at that time, so these connections began to materialize in private chat rooms where a bond would be formed between individuals who lived perhaps thousands of miles from each other.

As we researched this new phenomenon, we discovered that emotional connections often formed well in advance of any real in-person meeting. People we interviewed would tell us that they had fallen in love with someone halfway around the world through chatrooms and emails. At some point, inevitably, people finally had to meet in person. I jokingly thought that the airlines must have seen an uptick in domestic and international reservations as this new way of meeting was going through an explosive growth period.

In our book *Affairs of the Net,* we accurately predicted that online dating would be a popular way of meeting people and not just a passing fad. Since then, the numbers of online dating services catering to every conceivable demographic and preference have dramatically increased.

Some people do successfully meet this way. I recently received an email from one of the individuals whose stories we followed in the book. He reached out after many years to let us know that, after twenty-five years of marriage, they were doing great after having met in those early days online. For most people, however, the hype overplays the reality. There are multiple casualties in cyberspace, where vulnerable individuals are easily targeted and deceived. Unethical people troll for potential partners with the idea of financial gain or change in immigration status. Women are more likely to be such targets.

Other online relationships began with lies. Among them were married individuals claiming to be single, persons who lied about their gender, and of course, the one that is ubiquitous to this day, lies about age.

In any event, like it or not, internet dating is the primary medium today for meeting potential partners. Profiles posted online are supposed to give potential matches a great deal of information from which to decide if people want to proceed. In theory, much of the guesswork in getting to know someone is taken out of the equation. Unfortunately, so are the imagination and anticipation that go along with meeting someone and allowing the relationship to evolve organically.

I wonder how many potentially successful relationships never evolved because someone decided not to reach out because of a single, erroneously interpreted variable.

Let's get back to social climate change. How we interact with each other as human beings has undergone a radical departure from what we once knew.

I am going to shatter a myth right now. If you in any way believe that texting, emails, videoconferencing, or any other technologically mediated communication is just as good as face-to-face interaction, I challenge that notion.

Texting or messaging is the dominant mode of modern communication. There are no nonverbal cues to help us identify the message's context. The fact is that nonverbal communication accounts for a great deal of human interaction. With online or text exchanges, there is no tone of voice or range of affect to guide you. You cannot see the other person, so you can't judge any physical reaction to something you said.

A delay in response is also easily misinterpreted. Is the other person angry with me or just busy? The list of misinterpretations is endless.

Factor in also the devolution of grammar and language. Acronyms and improper syntax dominate communication and seemingly reflect our national impatience.

Texting is unquestionably a convenient and immediate method of communicating information. It definitely has its upside, and most of us use it several times a day. However, remember the dramatic difference between simply confirming a doctor's appointment with a one-word electronic response and dealing with an important interpersonal issue. The former is convenient, while the latter is meaningful and deserves proper attention.

If it is crucial, meet face-to-face or at least call. It will cut down on misinterpretation and have a fluid tempo.

Another profoundly impactful medium of connectivity is videoconferencing. The ability to hear and see another person anywhere around the globe is remarkable. It allows us to address those nonverbal aspects of communication I mentioned earlier.

Videoconferencing has created an opportunity to work, learn, and socialize from the comfort of your home. Your smartphone adds the convenience of maximum mobility. Yet not experiencing each other in three dimensions also has a cost, as an example from my practice demonstrates.

The pandemic has changed how we interact in dramatic ways, including doctor's visits. As things began to change, more and more appointments were segued to virtual meetings. I followed suit by offering my clients three choices. They could continue with a telemedicine call that included video or was audio only, or if they preferred, they were still welcome to come into my office, and we would follow sensible precautions. I would estimate that 75 percent still wanted to come in person.

Comfort and safety were my top priorities, but truthfully, I was pleased, for therapeutic reasons, that many people wanted to continue our sessions in person. My office has been carefully designed to enhance a client's well-being by taking advantage of nonverbal cues. From the moment someone enters my waiting room, they are met with soft piano music playing. Since I work precisely on time, rarely is anyone in the waiting area. My diplomas and framed covers of my books are strategically hung to enhance credibility.

My consulting room is warm and inviting. There are few places these days where you can experience some level of comfort and a respite from our hectic world. Every item in the office has a purpose. A prominent wooden bowl on the coffee table holds an abundance of mints. The three boomerangs of ascending sizes on the coffee table that sits between my chair and the proverbial couch imply we have opportunities for change but that repeated mistakes come back to us. I can occasionally gaze at a signed copy of a promotional cast picture from my favorite film, *The Wizard of Oz*. Dorothy reminds me of what is innocent and good in a tumultuous world.

All these elements come together to create a safe environment where the most effective therapy can take place. In treatment, the relationship between doctor and client is primarily based on trust. If a client experiences genuine care and concern in the presence of professional expertise, then a solid foundation is established so we can get to the challenging work ahead. If all these elements mentioned above are missing, then there is a high likelihood of losing helpful, nonverbally communicated information.

With couples, for instance, I may notice that one of the parties is slowly turning their wedding ring around when they are talking about an issue. Or they may sit at opposite ends of the couch and put a pillow or two between them. If someone breaks down and their partner demonstrates no empathy, I file that away. Tears of sorrow call for tissues, and a box is within easy reach of both myself and the client(s). If the partner doesn't reach for them after a minute or so, I will. Everything tells me something as I pay attention.

Someone may leave a personal article behind, like a pair of sunglasses or, more often, a set of keys. You might think of it as a simple act of forgetfulness; on the other hand, perhaps it's a positive sign that the client didn't want to leave.

If I am working with an older depressed client who prefers interaction by phone only, I can't see what's happening with their appearance and personal hygiene, which are important diagnostic data points. You get my point.

Moving on to everyday living, we all witness daily the degree to which our smart devices interfere with regular human interaction. Text and phone interruptions are the norms.

It seems that it's no longer socially unacceptable to have a full-on private conversation about virtually anything in the public arena. Even worse, whoever is within listening distance is by default welcome to listen in. My observation is that the more important someone thinks they are, the more they want to share that with strangers. Either that, or they have no situational awareness.

Not only that, but a new type of thief steals from each of us. These thieves are taking something away from us that we can never recover. Time is a nonrenewable resource. Endless spam calls and emails are problematic issues. Aside from the few seconds it takes to deal with an unwanted text, call, or email, the other element to contend with is distraction. One can be momentarily distracted from a conversation, train of thought, or much more seriously, attending to something important like driving a car or caring for a child. How important is all this in the scheme of things? Especially important.

Beware of the erosion of meaningful human interaction.

The more the quality of our interactions are affected by distractions and fast-paced, incomplete communications, the poorer the quality of those interactions. The probability of misunderstandings increases dramatically—and misunderstandings are at the root of much of America's mental health situation.

More than anything, people want to be listened to and understood. If someone does not receive the time and interest needed to connect in a richly human way, that can lead to frustration and aggression. Those results in turn fuel a type of psychological isolation and potentially damaging behavior.

Technology runs the risk of expanding the distance between people as opposed to decreasing it.

The degradation of quality human interaction is a major contributing factor as to why many Americans have a low threshold of frustration tolerance toward others. The simple axiom runs like this: the more in depth that you know someone, the more likely you are to understand their perspective.

THE ADDICTION TRAP

One of the most cherished aspects of living in America is the promise of freedoms that much of the world does not enjoy. The freedoms of speech, movement, and behavior have been a beacon for people worldwide since the beginning of this nation. These freedoms were not always available to all because of discrimination, though efforts throughout our history reflect a desire to correct inequalities.

Traveling around the world can give one a sense of just how privileged we are to live our lives as we please.

My wife and I were in Dubai a few years ago enjoying dinner when the individual bussing our table engaged us in a brief conversation. He was supporting his family, who lived in another country far away. Somewhat jokingly, or not, he asked if he could hide in our suitcase and come home with us. It was one of many signature moments that helped me appreciate how fortunate we are to live in this country. Anyone who has traveled beyond our borders to nations without our rights, privileges, and opportunities have had similar experiences.

My own family emigrated to the United States from Sweden a few years after World War II. For my parents, America offered a vision of hope and prosperity, and most important, the promise of a new life. Having endured five years of German occupation in the Netherlands and a complete loss of personal freedoms, they felt excited and blessed to have a new beginning. They also arrived with abundant gratitude that the Americans and their Allies had liberated their home country.

Personal freedoms, however, have another side: we can overindulge in them to our heart's content in almost every aspect of life.

Addictions of all kinds are epidemic and completely out of control. Much of what follows will seem obvious, but not so apparent is that these addictions are an insidious force that is ultimately weakening America.

No matter how much we spend on defense, the fact is that America is destroying itself from within. I do not make this assertion lightly. The obsession with outside threats such as terrorism is an interesting example of how we are missing the point.

No one would argue that ensuring our safety is a top priority. When I travel, I see the necessity of ensuring that my flight is as safe as possible. No one wants a repeat of 9/11.

Yet when observing the scene at the airport while waiting for a flight, I cannot help but notice that over half of my fellow travelers are obese or at least overweight. This reflects national statistics. Therein lies one of our country's real problems.

We are overeating ourselves to death. Heart disease, stroke, type 2 diabetes, and certain types of cancer are obesity related. Many more medical issues are linked to being overweight and practicing poor nutrition.

If there was one takeaway, I wish people would have learned from the pandemic that we are often the architects of our own undoing.

We have heard a lot about underlying conditions that have served as comorbid risk factors during the pandemic. That should be a major wake-up call. But taking it one step further, addictions fuel these underlying conditions.

Let me address something right now. People with addictions of all types use a very self-convincing defensive strategy known as denial. *Denial* is a way to rationalize one's behavior by convincing yourself that, for example, you won't be the one who gets sick or dies because of your addiction.

If you repeatedly tell yourself, *it will not happen to me*, you give yourself a pass to keep harming yourself.

Denial is a tried-and-true strategy to dismiss outright an objective reality. Unfortunately, we all use it to some extent at different points in our lives, but granting ourselves permission to engage in bad behavior is injurious because it's bad for you and, by extension, for everyone else.

For drug addiction—which includes tobacco, vaping, and alcohol addiction—I see these issues in my practice every day. Their destructive effects are genuinely catastrophic. Suffice it to say that if you are a reader directly dealing with these types of addictions—either yourself or with family members—you know firsthand how destructive they are (whether or not you are self-aware enough to admit the former). On the other hand, if you have been fortunate enough not to be affected personally, then I ask you to believe everything you've learned about how addiction ruins lives.

Drug and alcohol addiction are huge problems in America for individual lives and families. There is a loss of productivity, self-worth, and quality of life. Early death often results.

America has lost some of its sanity because, over time, what was once considered completely unacceptable has received tacit, if not express, approval. Alcohol is legal, readily available, and when used in moderation, can be an enjoyable part of life. Unfortunately, unchecked alcoholism or abuse can lead to many physical and psychological problems—for the alcoholics themselves and often for people around them.

Tobacco use wins the prize when it comes to harm. It remains the leading cause of preventable disease, disability, and death in the United States. Fortunately, the number of people who smoke has declined significantly and the number of quitters has risen. One reason is likely the well-accepted principle of social psychology. If smoking is considered less socially acceptable, there is a built-in motivation not to do it. If society has previously considered it cool to smoke, but now it's uncool, that helps.

Social comparison theory suggests that individuals determine some of their personal and social values by comparing themselves to others. Adolescents and young adults are especially tuned into what their peers are doing. The desire to fit in and be accepted is part of the rite of passage into adulthood. When self-image and self-esteem are evolving, the probability is higher of adopting a behavior that will end up being a lifetime addiction.

And now we have another alarming and problematic addiction. Vaping is the new lie. The inhalation of chemicals, including the primary ingredient of nicotine, into one's lungs under the pretense that the action isn't as harmful as smoking cigarettes simply isn't true. Because no unpleasant odor is released into the air, users are fooled into thinking that vaping is a benign activity. Since most e-cigarettes contain a pleasant (chemical) scent, the deception is further cloaked. While vaping hasn't been around long enough to determine its long-term physical effects, one can safely assume that it isn't good.

We also need to think about the legalization of marijuana and the introduction of medical marijuana cards. There are many legitimate uses for medical marijuana, most centering on helping individuals manage their pain, nausea, and other symptoms. Prescriptions are given out easily, though, for any complaint.

I am not here to argue the merits or dangers of unrestricted marijuana use, but let's be realistic. A substantial number of Americans of all ages abuse marijuana regularly. It can and does detrimentally affect motivation, and if you couple its abuse with gaming, you have all the makings for an uninspired individual.

Ease of access is always a factor in addiction rates. The availability of drugs to young adults translates into an earlier start-up age when addictions take root. Consider also that psychological development is typically stunted as a function of addiction. Moreover, some drugs serve as gateways to more serious substances.

This is tricky ground. I do not believe that criminalizing people who abuse drugs is helpful to anyone in the long run. But what about drug dealers and especially those who traffic hard drugs? A distinction needs to be made. Since hard-drug addiction is dangerous to individuals and society, purveyors should be held accountable.

Time for another anecdote. While on a trip to Singapore with my wife, upon entry we were given a customs declaration form that included a bold red disclaimer that stated that trafficking illegal drugs into their country was punishable by death. I read that over a few times, and it gave me pause. At first, I was shocked by the intensity of that simply stated warning. Then I began to think about what they were trying to protect. While certainly a harsh approach, the exceptionally low rate of drug abuse in their country is something to recognize.

We are all aware of the catastrophic effects of opioid addiction. I've avoided endless statistics in this discussion, but an exception should apply in this case. Fentanyl overdose deaths in America alone top one hundred thousand people every year. Think about that. In just ten years, we will have lost over one million of our fellow citizens to this one chemical.

Painkillers, cocaine, crack cocaine, heroin, benzodiazepines, stimulants, inhalants, and barbiturates round out our list of commonly abused classes of drugs.

The last addiction I mention is one we touched on earlier. Tech-based addictions of all kinds are hurting America.

Excessive time spent on *anything* that diverts our attention from living a balanced life hurts this country. All it takes is enough people being distracted to create a climate of superficial living.

Let's use an example. You've seen just how nonpresent people can be in a public setting. Haven't you observed a dinner table full of people staring at their smartphones? Maybe you've done that yourself. Or you've unwittingly found yourself listening to a private conversation because the person within earshot seemingly doesn't care or perhaps wants people to hear it. These situations may seem inconsequential, but they're not.

Human connectivity is rapidly being replaced by increasing dependence on nonhuman interfaces to fulfill connectivity needs. Whatever is programmed for your consumption competes for your attention.

These behaviors may seem benign, but as they become more socially acceptable, especially in public, we will be paying less and less attention to the person—or the stopped car—right in front of us.

Addictions need constant attention, so the pressure builds to feed the monkey, as soon or as often as possible. The monkey is the internet, and the drugs of choice are in endless supply.

As stated previously, gamers are particularly vulnerable as the reward structure of video games stimulates the same parts of the brain as do drugs. Dopamine release results in a high, and the chemical does not distinguish among its sources.

I am not suggesting a doomsday scenario, but dependency on technology for our entertainment and socialization will likely increase over time. Conversational artificial intelligence (AI) is becoming more sophisticated. As programs learn more and more about you and all of us together, customized responses will increasingly create the illusion that someone human is on the other end.

That's a very seductive concept as it depends on the suspension of disbelief. It's like watching a movie. You know it is a movie, but at the same time, you need to buy into it to be to be able to enjoy the experience. The same holds true of artificial intelligence and the psychological concept of *habituation*, which means being continually exposed to an initially novel experience and becoming accustomed to it over time. We become *habituated*.

If we come to rely on AI for our social needs, we can quickly start to believe that the relationship between ourselves and AI technology is more real than it actually is.

It's not that we are at risk for truly believing that the voice or the chatty avatar on the other end is real in any animate sense. It's more that we begin to depend on it as an alternative to human interaction, and that's a lonely place to be.

Anything used in moderation is pretty much okay, but as we have learned, anything that has a high potential for pleasure will be sought after at every opportunity.

My prediction is that technology will never achieve the power to overtake our inherent need to be with each other fully. But at the same time, if we do not keep technology in check, we run the risk of living mediocre lives.

In a very real sense, while we might judge the unconnected few as living with a deficit, one can argue instead that the range and depth of their interactions are far richer.

VIOLENCE IN AMERICA

We need not spend any time convincing anyone that America has a serious violence problem. Unfortunately, it's not as rare as it once was to learn of a mass shooting of some type. Gang-related violence remains a significant problem. Individual acts of violence against someone known to the aggressor or not are rising. At this writing, homicide rates have increased at an all-time-high rate.

The genesis of violence has multiple causes that involve individual and sociological factors. It's a very complex issue that analysts can approach from many angles.

For our purposes, let's look at what is known as the *frustration-aggression model of aggression*. The theory has been around since 1939 and has been modified since then. At its core, this model holds that an individual or group acts aggressively if a pressing need is blocked in some way. Of course, not all frustrating mental states result in aggression, but frustration is necessary for violence to occur. This can easily lead to *scapegoating*, which happens when a person or group is blamed for the perceived wrongdoings of others. A simple example illustrating this concept is as follows:

The boss at work berates an employee. The worker, who fears losing their job, suppresses their anger and goes home. The frustration our worker experiences begins to boil over at some point. Their partner does something very minor that is irritating. The frustrated worker, not wanting to fight, yells at their child, who in turn scares the dog, who then runs after the cat, and the poor mouse is doomed. You get the idea.

If the source of the frustration can't be challenged, for whatever reasons, then the violence gets displaced onto an innocent target.

Multiple individual psychological factors enter the picture as moderator variables that inhibit or release violence. *Moderator variables* are those that create the conditions that influence a response. Certainly, not everyone who is frustrated acts out aggressively. Most people do an excellent job of keeping their anger in check. They've learned how to successfully channel their anger or how to suppress it. *Suppression* is the conscious act of pushing down an unpleasant emotion because acting on it verbally or physically is unacceptable. Healthy outlets, such as engaging in, and experiencing the universally accepted benefits of exercise, can help diffuse those negative emotions.

Tragically, America is viewed throughout the world as a country where violence is commonplace. We do look more than a little insane to others in this regard. When you have a combination of easy access to firearms, particularly those with a particularly lethal level of firepower, along with a highly unstable person who is frustrated for whatever reason, we have a perfect storm for violence.

We also can't ignore the profound gender differences in violent crime perpetration. Sexual crimes, which are acts of violence, are far more likely to be committed by men and their victims are female.

Historically, attention was directed toward the idea that the Y chromosome was responsible for aggressive behavior. You may recall from basic biology that the Y chromosome is the determinant of male sex organs. This view has proven to be overly simplistic.

Males commit the overwhelming majority of violent crimes in America. A professor once half-jokingly told our class that crime would be radically reduced if males in the age range of fifteen to twenty-five years old were drafted into the military or public service for a ten-year span. Preposterous for sure, but interesting.

Cultural values also play a significant role in the sources of violence. Our present culture often promotes the idea that other people are viewed as obstacles in the way of a goal. Fast-paced lives create a condition wherein we can become obsessed with getting from point A to point B. Consider the obvious example of traffic on the road. Unless you live in a rural or semirural area, you're likely to find yourself coping regularly with traffic that can be a source of major frustration. Other drivers aren't viewed as persons like yourself trying to get to a destination, but rather as objects in our way.

Let's extrapolate that to every other situation where we compete for resources. When time becomes scarce in our lives, stress levels can quickly escalate to elevated levels, leading us to believe that we have little or no control over the events around us. The problem is that we are moving too fast to absorb what is truly happening in our lives. As a result, people have little time to reflect, which means we are often dumbing down the very quality of life for all of us.

What does this have to do with violence? Not taking the time to carefully consider what is affecting us and why has a powerful influence on our mental state. Of course, it requires a rationally thinking person to work through frustrating life experiences and explore reasonable options. Managing frustration is a skill best developed at a young age and taught accordingly, but as adults we have many beneficial ways to cope with life's inevitable challenges.

As we've learned, frustration can lead to verbal and physical aggression. While predicting violent behavior is notoriously difficult, the best predictor ends up being past behavior. Someone who has a history of violence and for whom that inclination goes unchecked is much more likely to be violent again. A robust anger-management intervention program targeting first-offense violent individuals would be a helpful strategy to address this tragic social issue.

In all its iterations, the entertainment media has made violence in America a cultural centerpiece. Many video games are extremely violent in their content and the goals they set for their players. Films have become progressively violent over the years, and the news dances along a fine line between information and sensationalist entertainment.

The net effect of all this excessive exposure to violence is the established fact that people can become desensitized. With desensitization, other people become even more objectified, and other human beings are reduced to two-dimensional characters in the perpetrators' mind.

The fix? Minimize the message in the media that violence is a solution to problems. A clever writer can resolve conflict through other means. Excessive violence is like deafening music—the less creative, the more amplification. That's the fix but highly unlikely to happen. Instead, since violence is what sells ("If it bleeds, it leads"), be an outlier and take responsibility for your own consumption of whatever the media marketplace offers.

ACCEPTING PERSONAL RESPONSIBILITY

Once we've identified some of the major challenges facing our country, the natural question that follows is, *what can I as an individual do about it all?*

The short answer is that unless you are in a position of major influence or power, your ability to scale changes significantly is limited to your personal sphere, whatever that is. With this knowledge, it would be easy to fall into a depressive state where you believe that we as a nation are completely collapsing. If you trust all the negative media that constantly barrage us with doom and gloom, then it's hard to draw any other conclusion.

As I've pointed out, we have severe problems facing our country, but all is not lost. By now, you know my position on all this. Propaganda is deliberate and has its intended goal of pushing an agenda to get us to think one way or another. It's unbalanced and incomplete. When you truly understand this concept, it frees you to think independently.

The most important action we can take is accepting personal responsibility for our attitudes and behaviors. How we arrived at those attitudes and behaviors is a complex interplay involving multiple domains.

For clarity's sake, let's say that our starting point is where you are at this very moment. Yes, circumstances and life events have a profound impact, but if we're going to move forward, there needs to be some level of acceptance that where you are now is your starting point.

Staying stuck in the past or having fears about the future is easy. Spending too much mental energy on your past is a trap, though. We need to learn from our past, but that's not where we're living. I like to tell my clients that there's a reason a car's rearview mirror is so much smaller than a windshield. What is behind you is far less important than what is directly ahead.

We saw earlier the major problem that accompanies assessing blame and then punishing individuals, groups, or institutions. The blame game doesn't produce winners. This seems basic enough, but the truth is that many people have shifted from an independent mindset to one of dependence.

Coming back to my practice, you may have noticed that I refer to the people I see as "clients" as opposed to "patients." That's deliberate, as my approach encourages a sense of empowerment in which individuals view themselves as the primary agent to change something important in their lives.

As the expert witness, I guide and encourage as best I can, focused on the needs of the complex individual sitting across from me. No size fits all in my work, so each game plan must be customized to find the best path forward.

At the first session, my goal is to have the client know that we can find a way to help alleviate some of their stress. The mobilization of hope is central to this process. Certainly, life events can leave one with a sense of hopelessness and despair, but as I wrote in the introduction, the powerful act of listening and witnessing can be enormously helpful and even healing.

What exactly do I mean by accepting personal responsibility? It's rejecting any tendency to blame any other influences for our circumstances as being the sole reason we are in our present position. If you believe you're completely powerless, then you're trapped, unless you realize that surrendering is the first step in the recovery process when it comes to addictions.

Even in cases where depression is the dominant problem, we can always find something to give a person hope and a sense of mastery over even a small part of their lives.

Clinical depression is a very serious mental health issue, as are anxiety disorders. Unfortunately, we're seeing record numbers of individuals in all age groups suffering from these problems. What many of these disorders have in common is that the person who is struggling often believes they are helpless in their circumstances. Cognitive-behavioral therapy (CBT) is one powerful intervention technique that challenges false assumptions about oneself and works to replace them with more constructive self-talk. *Self-talk* is essentially the narrative we tell ourselves about how we are moving through life. It reflects our beliefs and experiences. Depending on the accuracy of our narrative, it can either help or hinder us.

In my practice, I immediately work on helping a person see that we will find a way to mobilize their sense of self-efficacy. *Self-efficacy* is the belief that the attainment of your own goals is dependent on your ability to achieve those goals. If you have a powerful sense of self-efficacy, you accept challenges with the understanding that progress will be closely aligned with effort.

The American spirit has long maintained that if you work hard, much can be achieved. The key ingredient is that the opportunity to succeed needs to be in place. In many countries, significant opportunity for advancement in any domain simply doesn't exist. And as with our other topics, things here can get tricky.

A desire to be cared for can easily undermine the motivation to be self-sufficient. If there is sufficient incentive not to work, then why would you want to? This isn't a political or economic issue I'm addressing, though it has those implications. It's a profound psychological one.

Satisfied needs don't motivate.

Let's go a little deeper. A sense of self-efficacy is a close cousin of what we psychologists term "locus of control." Locus of control can be divided into internal or external.

Someone who goes through life by relying on an *external locus of control* takes action toward achieving their goals because some outside motivator expects such achievement. Keeping a work schedule offers a simple example. If you want to keep your job, you follow the parameters the employer has set.

A person who responds to an *internal locus of control* is essentially an initiative taker. Such people don't need something or someone else to direct them or tell them what to do.

A system that rewards a lifestyle that doesn't even require minimum effort puts a considerable risk factor in place that can keep someone from living a fuller life and reaching their potential.

Human behavior is such that there is a strong pull to taking the effortless way out. If there's a shortcut available to us, we're likely to use it. Occasionally that's fine, but if that is a person's modus operandi of moving through life, then psychological development can be stunted, and learning is thwarted.

I had a young person contact me to see if I would accept her as a client. I always screen on the phone with a few preliminary questions to see if we are potentially a good fit. When I asked her for the reason she'd like to come in, she replied that she wanted me to write her a letter in support of her application for Social Security disability. When I inquired as to what her disability was, she replied, "Nothing really. I just don't want to work."

I let her know that I wouldn't be able to accommodate that request, but that if she did manage to find someone to help her out, and if the application was successful, her ability to work in the future would be compromised. Maybe I shouldn't have been surprised when she calmly responded, "No, that's totally okay. I never want to work."

I don't need to explain the problem here, but it's a helpful segue into my next point: self-esteem correlates with self-efficacy. This is Psychology 101. If we look at any child who accomplishes something involving effort, the joy on their face is evident. The encouragement and praise bestowed on that child for their achievement go a long way in building self-esteem and a sense of mastery. Any goal realized through our efforts reinforces our sense of positive self-worth throughout our lives.

I practice in an affluent part of the United States, and I often see parents who overindulge their children materially. Their children attend private schools and may themselves drive very expensive cars. That's a choice parents make, but I gently remind them that excessive rewards without effort create an expectation of wealth in the absence of effort. The likelihood is greater than not that their children will be subject to unrealistic expectations as adults.

Now's the time to introduce my other daughter, Dana.

Dana is a highly educated mother of two daughters. A few years ago, she decided with her partner that they wanted to live as independently and self-sufficient a lifestyle as possible. They traveled across the United States and purchased forty acres of raw land out west. They built a house on their own, put in solar panels, and piped in fresh water from a nearby spring up a hill using a gravity feed. Refrigeration was solved by a deep well that reaches the permafrost. They raise livestock and can their foods for the winter. My granddaughters are homeschooled and are allowed little time online. They are well-balanced and mannered. I'm impressed with their sensitivity toward nature and knowledge of the cycles of life.

Paradoxically, their life off the grid is arguably on the grid of what is basic to our fundamental human need to be in sync with nature. Nature is the most powerful healing force on the planet.

This isn't an attractive or available lifestyle to most people, but it is an excellent example of self-sufficiency and personal responsibility. They are entirely dependent on their own skill sets, and the area where they live is one where neighbors join together to help each other in need. They socialize together and celebrate landmark events, and the strength of their interpersonal bonds is palatable.

Truly embracing personal responsibility and rejecting a victim mentality are liberating actions.

THE OBSERVING EGO

This next concept that I'm introducing is one of the most important principles I cover in this book. I'd ask you to take your time reading this chapter as it holds the key to helping America restore some of its sanity.

What do I mean by the term "observing ego"? Essentially, the *observing ego* refers to that part of our conscious awareness that takes a step back to evaluate where you are in the world you inhabit. It's as if you're looking at yourself in more objective terms instead of simply responding to various stimuli in your world.

The capacity to develop your observing ego is a critical component of self-understanding. It requires honest reflection and a desire to develop insight into who and what you are. Insight is only achieved through a willingness to carefully examine your thoughts, beliefs, and actions. It's based on an honest self-appraisal.

We discussed personal responsibility in the previous chapter. If excess energy is spent on assigning blame to influences beyond us, then we will forever miss the opportunity to understand our own inherent ability to change.

As discussed, during my training, all my colleagues and I were strongly encouraged to begin psychotherapy. We welcomed the opportunity as it was an especially important part of our education as future practicing psychologists. Certainly, the fact that we were all drawn to the field in the first place was a major element in our desire to develop self-understanding. One of the key components of a successful therapy experience is collaborating with a well-trained therapist who thoroughly understands the complex dynamics that take place in a therapeutic relationship—and being on the receiving end promotes that understanding.

Let's get back to the observing ego. If you desire to understand yourself better, you need to develop a habit of self-reflection. In our fast-paced country, we might seem to have little time to take stock of who we are. Many people experience life as a proverbial hamster on an endless wheel of tasks and to-do lists, with only the occasional respite.

We appear to have precious little time to catch our breath, let alone find an opportunity for self-reflection. Unfortunately, when that time does become available, we often occupy it with mind-numbing distractions that leave us feeling briefly entertained but ultimately unfulfilled.

If you take the time to observe yourself, you'll find that the world is continuously streaming feedback to you on your behavior. Your interactions with others provide you with an enormous amount of information about yourself and how you move through the world. Of course, observing others with a careful eye and ear can help guide your own behaviors.

You might wonder how you believe others perceive you. Perhaps you claim that you don't care, but that's another matter altogether. For our purposes, let's assume you do care.

People you interact with constantly reflect your behavior back to you. Kindness, much more often than not, generates kindness in return. Similarly, aggression tends to produce a likewise response from others.

If you sincerely want to develop your observing ego, you need to be aware of your own defense structure. Psychological defenses are necessary constructs that allow us to exist in the social world. We can use many defenses to cope with uncomfortable emotions; some are fixed while others can be applied depending on the circumstances.

As discussed in the chapter on addiction, a drug-dependent individual who refuses to recognize their addiction can deny they have a problem, which in turn enables them to continue abusing their drug of choice.

If I find an extra item in my grocery bag that I'm sure I didn't pay for, I will tell myself that it's not worth going back, and the store can afford the small loss. Rationalization is a handy defense.

Defenses protect us, but at a potential cost. You can easily short-circuit an experience that may have been beneficial somehow. Let's say that you're a person who is overly sensitive to criticism of any kind. If you readily reject feedback that might provide you with insights into yourself, you may be selling yourself short by missing a learning opportunity.

Learning from others requires an openness to accepting feedback and good listening skills. Often during an interchange, especially one with the potential for conflict, a person is already preparing their next sentence as a rebuttal. Not surprisingly, the quality of the exchange deteriorates rapidly, because the person is not engaged in active listening.

As Americans are more polarized than ever on various issues, it's easy to see that constructive dialogue is a major casualty in this zero-sum game. Individuals with a well-developed observing ego understand themselves as agents capable of change as they are open to internally and externally generated feedback.

If you find yourself in a polarized mindset, I'd ask you to explore your thoughts and feelings and decide for yourself as to whether your conclusion is genuinely your own or those that have been marketed to you. Again, this is where the ability to think with critical analytic skills in conjunction with an observing ego gives you an edge.

One more point: a person who is willing to engage in self-examination is also open to changing course when presented with new information about an issue. Unfortunately, many people are trapped in a state of cognitive dissonance. *Cognitive dissonance* occurs when a person finds themselves in a state of tension due to a conflicting thought or emotion. It's often generated through exposure to added information that conflicts with an earlier decision. To reduce that tension, one can simply reject the latest information or explain it away.

If you're unwilling to accept added information that goes against your original belief, then you may be missing an important opportunity to change direction. It's like being a passenger on the *Titanic* and believing the captain when he says, "Yes, we're taking on some water, but isn't it a beautiful evening?" If you think the ship is truly unsinkable, you might ignore the reality of the situation until it's too late.

Think for yourself and be open to change. Adaptation is an important condition that ensures survival when used properly.

IN SEARCH OF THE COMMONSENSE GENE

We all hear about the remarkable breakthroughs in understanding our genetic codes. One fascinating area of research has to do with behavioral genetics. Are our personalities set in stone when we're born or the result of developmental influences? The classic nature-versus-nurture question seems to always arise when seeking to explain why we are a certain way.

The simple truth is that our personalities are an extraordinarily complex interplay of genetic and experiential factors. The degree to which these factors are influential in personality development is likely to vary widely between any two people. When I'm asked if a particular attribute or trait is the result of nature or nurture, I always reply with, "The answer is 'C': both of the above."

At the same time, we are born into the world with certain individual proclivities. The obvious fact of gender is a powerful influence on how we move through the world. Even though there is a strong push during these times to neutralize gender, the fact remains that, for most people, gender differences are hardwired.

While society has come a very long way in acknowledging same-sex relationships, we need to be careful with introducing the transgender concept to children who are not psychosexually developed enough to understand the implications. Are we to believe that a massive latent number of children have been secretly yearning to change their gender? It would be wise to wait until a young person reaches the age of eighteen when they can decide as adults. One of the main reasons is the fact that adolescents often just want to fit in with their peers by standing out in some rebellious fashion.

One of the primary tasks in the rite of passage from childhood to young adulthood has to do with the process of *separation-individuation*, which refers to the intrapsychic process whereby an individual detaches from a primary love object, such as parents, in order to establish an independent identity. That identity is subject to many influences.

There seems to be a shortage of common sense in America these days. By "common sense," I'm referring to the acquired knowledge gained through life experiences that results in sound, measured judgment that others who have common sense can readily recognize. Everyday examples of common sense abound.

Here's an example of what I've viewed on the streets as a common-sense challenge to our sensibilities. On more than a few occasions, I've seen a motorcycle rider stopped at a light with a mask on to minimize exposure to a virus, but the operator isn't wearing a helmet. Somehow the threat of the virus is perceived as being much greater than that of having an accident that can result in a serious or fatal head injury.

Common sense would seem to dictate that the danger from an accident is far greater than picking up a virus in the open air on the highway.

Common sense loops back into life experience. If digital distractions replace real-life experiences, then good luck. The opportunity to develop sound judgment is compromised, which results in a problem in adapting to everyday experiences that require quick and rational decision making. Formal training isn't needed, which is why Grandma's advice was usually based on a lifetime of experience. Unfortunately, with America's obsession with youth, elders' opinions are typically dismissed or marginalized. As a result, we are missing a great resource by not tapping into the wisdom that older people have accumulated.

We will never identify a commonsense gene, but if we really want to make America sane again, we need to embrace a philosophy that elevates the value of sound judgment as a function of life experience. It starts with our children.

I like to say that smart people learn from experience, and really smart ones learn from the experience of others.

KINDNESS AS A FORCE MULTIPLIER

The survival of our species depends on cooperation. As much as Americans embrace a philosophy of independence, the reality is that, without exception, we are all interdependent. Everything that we rely upon for our well-being results from others working on our behalf. We don't think much about who grows our food or brings it to market. The electricity or gas we use comes from somewhere, right?

Being aware that others are helping to support our lives in complex ways is a starting point in developing gratitude, and gratitude is closely related to a state of contentment. Unfortunately, genuine happiness is in short supply for most Americans.

We touched earlier on the idea of scapegoating. As a reminder, it's the idea that we can take out our frustration on an innocent party. With all the stress in our country, the conditions exist for short tempers and aggressive acts that are entirely out of proportion to the perceived injury. So what can be done to mitigate anger and dissension?

The fact is that kindness is a force multiplier. It benefits both the sender and receiver. Life is challenging enough without making it harder on each other by being rude or demeaning.

Here's a psychological axiom that you can be sure of: **any stressful life event is best mediated through social support**. If you have a solid social support system in the form of family, friends, or a group, you are much better off than someone who is isolated. It makes common sense.

Kindness in our interactions with others generally brings us closer together. Being difficult pushes people away. If you choose to affiliate with like-minded angry people without any constructive goal in mind, you are simply solidifying your anger.

What I mean by *kindness* is the deliberate and intentional act of caring for others in word or deed. This is especially needed now, when hostility can be free-flowing and one's aggression, particularly online, is easy to indulge. The expression of anger is becoming a social norm, and that's seriously undermining America's mental health.

Kindness is best achieved through tolerance. When we're tolerant toward others, we acknowledge their differences without being threatened by them. We should have zero tolerance for many things in life, such as abuse. Most situations, though, lend themselves to understanding and acceptance.

When you act with kindness in the face of anger, something interesting happens. Very often, the person with the calm demeanor now controls the situation. An inverse relationship between exists kindness and aggression. The more thoughtful and calmer you are, the more you control the outcome—not always, but often enough.

Kindness has a strong pulse. I have spent my professional life as a psychologist listening to a vast array of problems that characterize the struggling side of the human condition. One might think that a career that involves so much exposure to stressful life events might lead to a pessimistic outlook. Fortunately, that's never been the case. I have been blessed with the opportunity to see firsthand that in a world that can be unhinged, acts of kindness appear all the time and often in the most unlikely ways. What follows is a personal example.

Meagan's primary care physician referred her to me to treat stress associated with retinitis pigmentosa, a progressive genetic disorder resulting in eventual blindness or near blindness. Before we continue, take a moment to imagine going blind. It's not pleasant. Try to wonder what it must be like to slowly have your vision stripped away. At first, you notice that your night vision and peripheral vision are affected. Over time, tunnel vision develops to the point that you are completely unable to determine what is immediately to your left or right. Eventually, the world is a blur at best, and all of what you took for granted—driving, reading, recognizing a face—becomes a memory. Considering that this particular sense accounts for over 80 percent of the information we take in about our world, losing one's sight is nothing short of a personal tragedy. Hold on to that thought.

Before her diagnosis, Meagan was a successful businesswoman, social, and in her words, "a completely different person." When I met her, I soon discovered that she cared for her live-in mother, who has advanced dementia. A part-time aide provided what little help she was able to secure. It was easy to sense that she'd been transformed from a woman who confidently moved through the world to someone whose life had become dominated by stress and despair.

At one point, she told me in passing about a recent technological device that, attached to a pair of ordinary-looking clear glasses, could help visually impaired individuals navigate the world. A small camera could read print, determine colors, and identify and store faces—all of this information and more would be shared with the user through a discreet earpiece. Meagan had even experienced how it worked when a social service agency demonstrated it for her. She lit up when describing what it could do for her. Unfortunately, it cost thousands of dollars and was financially out of reach.

I gave it some thought and asked Meagan's permission to see if I could help her find a potential financial resource without giving out any personal specifics, and she reluctantly agreed. I knew from working with her how difficult it was for her to accept help. That evening, while sharing Meagan's story with my wife, Suzanne, she listened carefully, said very little, and I thought nothing more of it. The next day, Suzanne simply announced that she had thoroughly researched the device and validated its value through multiple sources. Further, she had identified and established a funding network.

It was an exciting moment, and I couldn't wait to hear her plan. "We are going to buy the device for her, and my mother is in on it." It was said in her matter-of-fact tone, but her smile gave her away. She added, "To whom much is given, much is expected." Before I had time to react, she explained, "I ordered it already, and they will be over to her house to train her within the next few days." We would buy Meagan a voice-activated smart concierge device while we were at it. We felt blessed that we were given this opportunity to help in such a meaningful way and decided that even if her life improved just a little bit, it was well worth it.

It took some convincing, but Meagan gratefully accepted what we offered. Within a week, she came into her appointment and demonstrated the new device. It was very impressive, and she let me know that the new virtual assistant allowed her to access all kinds of information through voice commands. As it turns out, an unforeseen benefit is that her mom loves listening to Frank Sinatra during the day. It seems dementia hasn't stopped her from enjoying music. Meagan's struggles continue, but life is a bit easier than it was. Mission accomplished.

My career has left me pretty battle-hardened when it comes to expressing my own emotions, but I will admit that, though Meagan couldn't see them, my own eyes welled up with tears when she cried in my office that day. I'm sure she did hear my voice crack a bit when I told her the blessing was ours to be able to help her.

Opportunities to express kindness and receive it are all around us. It only takes the right attitude to enrich others and ourselves. It simply comes down to this: do you want to spread positive or negative energy to others? Either choice has significant psychological consequences. You decide.

IS OPTIMISM ON LIFE SUPPORT?

Imagine this if you can. The day is November 12, 1954, and the place is Ellis Island, New York. The island is famous for having processed more than twelve million immigrants into the United States. I was barely two years old at the time, and my family was aboard a ship that had just arrived from Europe. Amazingly, we were processed on the very last day the Ellis Island center was open before it was shut down forever.

My parents welcomed the opportunity to begin a new life in America. They had endured five years of Nazi occupation in the Netherlands, and arriving in a country with an abundance of food and goods with no bombed-out buildings must have seemed unreal at first. I would hear many stories of their wartime experiences over the years, but what stood out for me was their gratitude for all the Allies who had liberated their country. To this day, Dutch families adopt a veteran's grave with a pledge to take care of it.

America held the promise of a better life for my parents and millions of others. It was a place unlike any other in the world. The opportunity to achieve success and live in a country where one could believe in anything without persecution was a dream. Every immigrant to America arrives with hope and a sense of optimism—the common denominators of all who come here.

Unfortunately, a seismic shift seems to be occurring in this country from an energetic optimism to a sharp rise in negativity and pessimism. You certainly know what I'm talking about here. It's apparent in our day-to-day conversations on virtually any topic that touches on politics, the economy, or other issues that the media addresses.

We are not living in a binary world, but it would seem so. Once again, I'm warning you not to take a deep dive into all the negativity that very likely surrounds you. While many troubling issues are deeply concerning, those issues need to be addressed in a constructive way.

This is where you come in. The challenging work is understanding that most problems we're facing as a nation are highly complex. The desire to simplify our understanding of those issues can lead us to false conclusions that color our worldview. Most issues are not black or white. They're gray. Trust me on this, as I've spent forty-plus years in the gray zone of human behavior. Of course, it's very foggy in there sometimes, but that's the reality.

So is optimism on life support? That depends on your attitude. If you are susceptible to all the relentless negativity surrounding you, you might believe America is becoming a lost cause. On the other hand, your vantage point could be very different if you're tuned into your observing ego.

If you're willing to take a close look at where you individually stand in the optimism–pessimism continuum, I have an exercise in mind for you. You will need to focus on this one. Here we go:

Try not to think about politics for a moment. That might be tough since it's such a dominant force in our daily lives. Don't think about anything other than your individual life experiences. I want you to focus on your relationships with family, friends, coworkers, and even strangers. How would you rate the quality of those relationships? Of course, they vary by person, but I would venture to say that most of them lean toward the positive side of the relationship continuum. Why is that? Because we're social beings and want to get along. Your interactions with others are mostly positive or benign.

Now I'll go out on a limb: most people are good. Yes, difficult individuals and even psychopaths are out there, but they're rare. By "good," I simply mean that intentions are positive, and goals are reached through cooperation, not antagonism.

Now let's expand the concept to suggest that that our interactions throughout society are overwhelmingly benign or positive. With a population of over 330 million people, we can do some simple math and discover that tens of billions of interactions occur every day.

These interactions, brief or not, are overwhelmingly positive, and there you have it: **we're getting along better than you might think**. This isn't newsworthy, but it should be. Now let's take another step and consider the fact that Americans are among the most charitable people on the planet. They donate more money and volunteer more time per capita than people in every other country on earth. I'm not talking about government spending here, but individual citizens digging into their own pockets to help others in need.

Beyond monetary help, Americans volunteer more of their own time helping others than anyone else. Americans are good people, and charity is associated with hope and optimism that those in need may be lifted out of their plight into a better place. Charitable deeds don't get much play these days, but they abound.

If optimism is on life support, you're the cure.

NO PERSON LEFT BEHIND

A major mental health issue facing our nation is that many Americans suffer from social isolation. I see this in my practice daily. Loneliness is correlated with a multitude of physical and psychological issues. The simple reason, as we've been discussing, is that humans are inherently social. We depend on interpersonal connections for our survival and psychological well-being. Many other cultures worldwide place a much higher value on intergenerational bonds.

Additionally, we have always been a mobile society. Family and friends often live hundreds or thousands of miles apart. While technology now permits real-time video calls, it is shortsighted to say that they are equivalent to in-person meetings. There is no substitute for a hug, and we all know the value of human touch.

A number of studies have confirmed the commonsense understanding that the sensory deprivation resulting from a lack of physical contact can contribute to a number of psychological problems that can manifest later in life, especially if a human being is deprived of contact at birth. Bonding is a critically important developmental event.

One important effect of social isolation is damage to one's self-esteem. People who experience life as though they personally are unimportant live in a potent breeding ground for depression. This particular type of depression has to do with loss—often associated with health challenges that impair mobility but also with the loss of meaningful human interaction.

To feel valued, a person needs to sense that their life is important. This happens when someone reaches out in a caring manner. As we navigate the world around us, we see clearly that most of our social interactions are quickly dispatched and superficial. While that's often necessary in a fast-paced environment, it sacrifices quality exchanges.

Another problem with social isolation is that we can become self-centered without deliberately meaning to, as we subtly view our individual lives as more important than others. As I've said, this is especially true when competing for resources or trying to achieve a goal.

A few years ago, I learned a lesson I will never forget. I joined the army on Friday, September 14, 2001, at the age of forty-nine. Following the harrowing events of 9/11, I knew that we were in for some challenging times. I had to petition the army surgeon general for an age waiver, which was granted. My brief time in the army was definitely one of my richest life experiences, but that's another story.

I was completing basic army medical corps officer training at Fort Sam Houston in San Antonio, Texas. There we learned the basics of navigation, small arms weapons, medical evacuation, communications, and a host of other military-related skills.

We participated in various field exercises that certainly tested my adaptive skills. One such activity involved donning MOPP gear under a simulated gas attack. "MOPP" stands for "Mission Oriented Protective

Posture" and refers to protective equipment used in a toxic environment such as exposure to chemical, biological, radiological, or nuclear threats.

Once the warning, 'Gas, gas, gas!" is shouted out, the idea is to don the cumbersome suit, including hood and gas mask, as quickly as possible.

The exercise came right after being exposed to CS gas in a concrete bunker. CS gas is tear gas. Every person who has gone through military training will never forget it. Tear gas is potent, and when they tell you that its effects are just a fraction of what real threats are out there, that gets your attention.

So here we were out in this field in the sweltering Texas July heat in full standard field gear, and the alarm is sounded. We all clumsily shed our equipment, suited up in our protective gear, and ran like crazy to the assigned rally point. The sergeant quickly inspected each of us to determine if we'd made a good seal with our equipment.

Satisfied, he looked us all over after taking our MOPP gear off, and then the bomb dropped.

"Good job, people. Look behind me." The tone of his voice telegraphed his disappointment. There we saw one of our fellow soldiers struggling with putting on his gear out in the field. I wasn't sure if this was a well-rehearsed response on his part or he was truly disappointed in us. I'm sure he'd seen it many times before. It didn't matter; we'd screwed up.

"Did you look around and check on your buddies to see how they were doing after you finished protecting yourself?"

We were a good group. Cohesive, friendly, and working cooperatively on every other task, but this was a wake-up call.

Our silence was deafening as he knew that we all realized he was right.

Lying in my bunk that night, it occurred to me that the tear-gas exposure before the MOPP exercise might not have been a coincidence. I had learned that every single detail of training had a purpose.

My conclusion was that since we're hardwired to avoid pain and discomfort, even the *idea* of being gassed was enough to motivate us into donning our gear as fast as humanly possible. Even though the threat was artificially contrived, the net effect was one where we failed to scan our surroundings to see if anyone else needed assistance.

We all felt bad and apologized to our fellow soldier for neglecting to help. He was a great sport about it all, and it was not something a few beers at the officers' club couldn't fix.

Try to be aware of anyone within your reach who may be isolated and lonely. Reaching out to them is a gift that enhances the receiver and the givers' lives. The more bonded we are, the more our social fabric as a nation is strengthened.

Remember the phrase "United we stand, divided we fall."

OPEN YOUR TOOLBOX

You already know what you need to do to care for yourself. Hopefully, you're already doing it. In case you need a refresher:

- Don't smoke.

- Exercise regularly.

- Don't do illicit drugs.

- Keep a healthy weight for your height and build.

- Limit news exposure and think for yourself.

- Be kind toward others, especially strangers.

- Be patient with yourself and others.

- Cultivate a non sarcastic sense of humor.

- Be tolerant.

- Honor the spiritual side of your life.

The first four on that list are difficult behaviors to change if we struggle with addictive tendencies. The last six are immediately within your control. Attitude is key.

Most of us have habits we'd like to change, but two things need to happen. First, we need to be aware of the behavior that needs modification or elimination. The best outcome occurs when we've managed to replace a maladaptive pattern with one that is much better for us and other people we encounter. Conscious awareness is an essential component of behavior change. We either come to that awareness through our own self-reflection or when others point it out to us. The second component is to change the target behavior. Most behaviors take a few months to change, but that depends on many variables. Everyone is different.

Let's take losing weight as a common concern. People have often read and heard a smorgasbord of diet advice over the years, much of it conflicting. And they still expect that the next book will finally reveal the information they've been seeking.

The truth is that someone interested in losing weight already knows what steps to take. Gathering more information is simply a form of procrastination, an obstacle in itself to overcome. Information mining becomes another unconscious reason not to do something. It's a form of resistance. That we'd resist acting on something good for us doesn't seem to make sense, but it fits easily within the bounds of human psychology. Self-sabotage is ubiquitous.

The same principle applies to the list of obvious directives you just read regarding your toolbox. **The secret sauce, of course, is motivation**, which is where the observing ego comes in handy again. If you honestly take stock of yourself in as objective way as possible, you will be ahead of the game when accepting personal responsibility.

We talked about the blame game, which gets us nowhere. Accepting personal responsibility is a necessary condition for change but not a sufficient one.

Needs that satisfy may no longer motivate you, so you must reach for something higher. You have to care enough about yourself, though. If you don't care, we've reached another issue to address.

Let's dive into the weeds on this one. People who have no hope or faith in themselves run a real risk of living unfulfilled lives. I'm not talking about the usual indices of success here either. This isn't about money, power, or status. It's about being a member of society who contributes to its welfare.

John F. Kennedy said in his inaugural address, quoting Cicero, "Ask not what your country can do for you but rather what you can do for your country." His thinking underscores the belief that we all have a role in the betterment of America. Unfortunately, many people have become too self-centered and preoccupied only with their own needs and desires.

If you reach into your personal toolbox and try your personal best to take care of your physical and psychological self, you will have helped to ensure your place as a healthy member of American society. The added benefit is that you can take pride in knowing you are part of the solution, not the problem.

Yes, it's that simple.

THE WORLD IS NOT FLAT

While two massive oceans separate the United States geographically from much of the world, there's no question that we are more part of a global community than at any other time in history. Internationally scaled issues that affect virtually every person on earth, directly or indirectly, increasingly demand cooperation if they are to be managed overall. During challenging times, we have an opportunity to gain experience from each other. Travel especially affords us the chance to experientially learn about diverse cultures.

Management of stressful events is mediated through accepted societal values and behaviors. In this chapter, we sample some best practices by looking at countries from different regions of the world and how they cope with stress. We start by sharing an attitude and a few practical suggestions from those countries. Pay close attention, as the world offers some great ideas to reflect on and apply to your own life.

JAPAN

The Japanese people tend to view life in more temporal terms. Their understanding is that stressful events will end over time. In doing so, there is comfort in the knowledge that life events can be seen from an observational point of view. We covered this critical concept earlier when we explored the concept of the observing ego.

By taking a philosophical approach to stress, there's less of a cultural tendency to be reactive and more of an ability to view events from what I like to term is a higher altitude.

The ability to gain perspective allows an individual to see that others are experiencing the same stresses. This leads to empathy, which in turn strengthens the two-way bonds between people.

Social-emotional support encourages self-discipline, which is highly valued in Japan.

Tips from our Japanese friends:

- Take a daily, long relaxing soak in the tub.
- Drink green tea. Make the preparation a ritual.
- Walk daily in nature.

FRANCE

People in France tend to not center their lives around work, money, or acquiring more and more material objects. Instead, they focus on savoring the small, everyday things that make up daily life. Most notably for the French, of course, is the preparation and enjoyment of tasty food in concert with conversation. Like the Japanese, the French emphasize enjoying the simpler things in life.

Tips from our French friends:

- Enjoy dessert with your meal or anytime the spirit moves you. You read that right. Savoring a cookie, pastry, cake, or ice cream is perfectly acceptable if the portions are small. The all-or-nothing approach to food and drink is replaced in France with an attitude of simple moderation.

- Dedicate a proper time and place for mealtimes without distractions. Mindfully savoring each bite of food is key.

- Walk at every opportunity. See a pattern here?

- Dress with pride. Paying attention to your appearance builds self-confidence.

- Read from a nondigital source.

- Practice some joie de vivre. Sitting outside in nature and doing nothing can be a powerful stress reducer.

BRAZIL

Brazilian culture places great emphasis on commitment to family. Bonds among relatives are strongly affirmed through caring for each other instead of being self-centered. This extends to the greater community outside the individual family orbit. The time-demonstrated philosophy that challenge is best managed through social support guides Brazilian behavior.

Brazilians generally understand that much of life can't be controlled, although our responses can be. This results in a posture of acceptance of certain circumstances instead of trying to alter factual events.

Tips from our Brazilian friends:

- Reach out to family and friends at every opportunity. Time spent socializing is a powerful tool that can mitigate stress.

- Celebrate any occasion. Brazilians love to get together for any reason, and they especially enjoy meeting new people. Remember that a stranger is a potential friend you haven't met yet.

- Enjoy the simple pleasure of bathing—the average Brazilian showers between two and four times per day.

THE NETHERLANDS

The Dutch have a work hard–play hard philosophy of life. They are highly industrious people who take their downtime seriously. Like the other countries we've touched on, interpersonal socialization ranks high in their stress management behaviors. On the other hand, they like to practice *niksen*. Niksen is quite simply taking time out to do absolutely nothing. There's no purpose to niksen other than just being. There is no goal or objective. It's not even a meditative state but one in which the mind is allowed to wander. If you've spent time in niksen, you should be able to claim very thoroughly to have been doing absolutely nothing. Of course, this concept can be challenging for anyone who believes that all time must "productive." I can't think of anything these days more productive than giving our minds some much-needed rest.

Our brains require time to recover from all the inputs received every day. While sleep is critical to mental and physical health, the importance of giving our minds a break during our waking hours is invaluable.

Tips from our Dutch friends:

- Gather with friends at their homes at first before going out.

- Spend an hour every day practicing niksen and discover for yourself just how satisfying a complete disengagement from work or leisure activities can be.

- When the opportunity is available, travel. The Dutch are big adventurers and travel whenever they get a chance. Exploring other places and cultures expands our reach and our understanding of divergent peoples, which has the profound effect of strengthening human bonds and transcending human differences.

Of course, when we review this small sample of countries from different regions of the world, we can see that most of these best practices involve socialization. As Americans, we would be well advised to try and adopt some of these highly effective natural stress management methods. Overconsumption of media, food, alcohol, and drugs isn't the answer.

PERSONALITY AND STRESS

Personality is an enormously powerful moderator variable with respect to how an individual responds or reacts to life stressors. Who you are as an individual determines in large measure how you experience any life event. This may seem obvious, but let's take a closer look at what may be a very limiting worldview.

We tend to journey through life believing that our experiences and, more important, our interpretation of these experiences reflect the world as it is. Perception is your reality, but over 7.79 billion perceptions of life are taking place simultaneously at this very moment.

Pause for a moment and consider that previous sentence. The fact that we share certain common realities reflects that we are more alike than not, though that tells only part of the story.

As a psychologist, I can attest to the fact that once you begin to explore the complexities of each individual human mind, you discover something truly extraordinary. We inhabit a world of individuals whose life journeys are unique and highly personalized. While we can appreciate that others live quite different lives than ours, that's primarily an intellectual understanding. From an experiential point of view, we see the world through our own personal lens and often run the risk of making attribution errors.

An *attribution error* is a fundamental misunderstanding of the motives that drive other people's behaviors. It refers to a tendency to attribute someone else's actions to their personality and our own actions to our circumstances. Think of it as a type of mental shorthand where we oversimplify complex behavior by categorizing someone according to a label of some sort. These errors contribute heavily to stress, reflecting a misjudgment of others and their motives.

Let's use a simple example of an attribution error. Suppose someone you know who is usually pleasant but who is acting irritably. You might think they're behaving this way because they're angry with you for some unknown reason. That may be true, but the real reason might be that they are ill, received some unwelcome news, or feel stressed. Remember that frustration leads to aggression. The best way to avoid an attribution error is to simply gather more information.

In contrast, if I find myself in an irritable mood, I'm more likely to ascribe my thoughts and behaviors to circumstances and not my personality; we're looking at another version of the blame game.

We can't know everyone in depth, of course, but the basic awareness that other people are extraordinarily complex can help us appreciate people's differences. We are always working with limited information, as people publicly show their social masks. A person's *social mask* is that part of themselves that they are willing to reveal to the world. In reality, it's the tip of the iceberg, concealing the complexity of what lies beneath their social selves.

It's an occupational hazard, but I often pass by strangers, even on the highway, and wonder about their backstories. They're undoubtedly rich in history. As I like to say, there are no boring stories, only boring storytellers.

Returning to our discussion of personality, our starting point is to recognize that personality is a psychological construct affected by age, gender, physicality, intelligence, culture, and developmental and other factors. How those variables interface with stressors has everything to do with how effective our coping mechanisms respond to threats.

Before we go any further, let's look at a good working definition of "stress." We hear the word all the time, but what does it mean?

Stress is any perceived threat to our natural state of homeostasis. Those threats can be either external, internal, or both. Some are universally perceived, while others are individually experienced.

A simple example of an external stressor is as follows: if you were out in the woods and suddenly confronted by a ten-foot grizzly bear, no doubt there would be an instant physiological and psychological response that anyone in that circumstance would share. Of course, not everyone would respond precisely the same way, but a stressor would be universally experienced. We'd be frozen in fear, run away as fast as possible, or try and distract it or attack it. You've heard of the fight-or-flight response, and we're all hardwired for that.

Other stressors are tailored to the individual, such as developing a phobia. Phobias are highly personal in the sense that what one person fears as a stressor is completely benign to another. The fear of public speaking is the most common phobia, but many people embrace talking in front of a group with pleasure. While the audience may be neutral or even friendly and receptive, the internal psychological perception of the environment would trigger a reaction for someone with such fear. People with phobias almost always recognize that their fears are objectively irrational, but their fight-or-flight mechanism takes over. There may not be a grizzly bear in the audience, but it sure feels that way for some people.

We can learn much from the personalities of people who are most effective in coping with stress. Here are the key characteristics:

FLEXIBILITY

Survival depends on adaptation. Changing strategies in the face of novel circumstances is a critically necessary component of a healthy personality. On the other hand, inflexibility can lead to heightened anxiety, affecting mental and physical health.

RESILIENCY

Healthy personality types have a greater ability to depend on their own initiative and view stressors as a challenge rather than an obstacle. They have the means to move forward in life no matter what they face.

Their attitude is not one in which they feel victimized or helpless. They have a powerful sense of internal locus of control.

LOCUS OF CONTROL

Simply put, external locus of control is the mindset in which an individual views events as externally dictated and may feel powerless as a result. This, in turn, creates a foundation in which anxiety and depression can thrive. The learned-helplessness model of depression asserts that some types of depression are caused by a person's belief that they are ineffectual at influencing outcomes, no matter what they do to change things. Considering our present experience with the pandemic, many people have believed they are helpless and found themselves waiting and hoping for this worldwide stressor to subside in its impact before engaging in any semblance of normality.

Individuals with an advanced internal locus of control approach events in a very different manner. They rely on self-efficacy, meaning that they size up a situation and determine how they can best respond to it by mobilizing resources they can bring to bear.

Persons with a high internal locus of control are realistic in their appraisals of what they can or cannot achieve. They don't have a naïve worldview but instead focus on what permits them to adapt in the best conceivable way. They also move through their lives with a powerful sense of personal responsibility.

PSYCHOLOGICAL HARDINESS

Psychological hardiness is a strong predictor of how well someone adapts to stressors. Mentally hardy individuals are stronger because they have a more stoic attitude toward life. They recognize that life can be complicated and even tragic, but they continue to move forward.

The ability to continue engaging as much as possible in regular activities helps normalize life and return an individual to a state of homeostasis. The attitude is one in which the psychologically hardy person decides that whatever the stressful event is, it will not change everything. Hardiness and flexibility go hand in hand.

SOCIAL CONNECTEDNESS

Personality types with a high need for social support and connectedness do well in times of stress. Therefore, the best predictor of how well an individual will weather any life stressors is how much social support they receive and give to others. Interacting with others has been particularly challenging during the pandemic. Therein lies a major problem.

Humans are social animals. We're programmed that way. Our inherent need to connect with others begins at birth and serves a basic survival function. Numerous studies and common sense assert that a failure to bond at birth can lead to significant developmental issues later in life.

Throughout our lives, we seek to affiliate with family, friends, and those with whom we share attitudes and interests. During any collective threat, the natural tendency is to aggregate, gather, and find support in groups. In terms of the pandemic, being required by law or social convention to practice interpersonal distancing and refrain from gathering in groups has come at a high cost.

From a mental health perspective, social isolation has had a devastating impact on a considerable part of the world's population. Individuals living alone in cultures with lower social connectedness indexes have been particularly affected. Loneliness is truly a killer.

Social media platforms that permit people to gather over the internet helped to mitigate some of the isolation. Internet based celebrations as well funerals became common events.

Another danger is associated with overreliance on social media. It can readily lead to a term I'm going to coin right here: "social anorexia."

Social anorexia is the subtle loss of quality human interaction through the misleading belief that online interactions contribute to the development of emotional intelligence. Online usage also contributes to a kind of laziness where complex human interactions are reduced to an image, short text, or post.

Some children and young adults who have been born into the internet age are especially at risk for social anorexia simply because they have had little chance to develop basic interpersonal face-to-face skills.

As discussed earlier, the importance of human touch cannot be overstated. The benefit to the immune system of a handshake or an embrace, physiologically and psychologically, is significant. Individuals with a high need for affection are particularly vulnerable to what can be described as "touch starvation."

When we are hungry or thirsty, that need isn't satisfied until we've had something to eat or drink. Over time, the lack of touch can become a need that, when unmet, can lead to depression and anxiety and contribute to a host of physical issues.

Individuals who are well connected to others and who are positively inclined develop a solid foundation of immunity to stress.

SENSE OF HUMOR

People with personalities that find humor in stressful experiences are better suited to put things in perspective. Taking things less seriously is a coping strategy that allows people to distance themselves and be less deeply affected. Humor is the ability to find a lighter prism through which to see the world.

There is nothing humorous about tragic events, though, and nothing funny about all the pain and suffering people endure. Humor at someone else's expense is never acceptable, nor is sarcasm. Sarcasm is related to pessimism and a negative worldview.

If you can get in touch with funny parts of your personality, then you can learn not to take yourself so seriously all the time. We are all imperfect beings when we index ourselves against social and spiritually based standards. An appreciation for those imperfections can provide us with fertile soil to make light of ourselves.

As an example, here's a self-reveal. I have obsessive-compulsive traits that dictate that my consulting room must be perfectly staged. If anything is out of place, I move it back into its perfect spot right in front of my client. I'm notorious for using coasters, so one has already been perfectly positioned when people put down a drink. We always have a quick laugh at that, and it serves two important purposes. One is to let them know I have a quirk (or two) of my own, so they feel comfortable knowing I also have issues. The second reason has to do with the meta-message that we shouldn't always take ourselves too seriously. It helps to humanize the therapy experience. The truth is that most issues that come through my practice are very serious and far from humorous. Still, it helps, if possible, to sometimes try and see the lighter sides of things.

THE SOLUTION

We've seen in previous chapters that much of the discord in this country is generated through a lack of understanding of the psychological principles that underlie our behavior. Once you thoroughly comprehend these principles, you'll be better equipped to navigate the complexity of living in contemporary America. I hope you now have a better appreciation for the forces acting upon you and your fellow Americans.

The problems are by no means minor. On the contrary, as we've seen, some serious challenges demand action if they are to be appropriately addressed.

No single individual or entity is to blame for the divide and polarization that exist, and trying to assign such blame is an oversimplification. Categorizing individuals as wholly "good" or "bad" does people a disservice.

My intention has been to emphasize personal responsibility for our attitudes and how they shape behavior. Once you become aware of the why, you can free yourself. The subtle and not-so-subtle forces in play that mold your worldview need to be kept in check, or you run the risk of becoming a casualty of propaganda.

If you want to heal yourself and, by extension, America, you need to climb to a higher altitude. The "higher altitude" I'm referring to is how we strive to be the best we can be as human beings. A higher altitude is a spiritual one where we can understand ourselves on a deeper level that transcends this earthly plane in which we're living.

Think of your spiritual self as an observing ego on steroids. In my experience, those individuals who embrace their spiritual selves tend to do better in coping with life's inevitable difficulties. I'm humbled by those who somehow face the most difficult of life's sorrows with a strength that transcends their circumstance.

We are all on a spiritual journey. I'm not asserting that based only on my own understanding of life and beliefs. I know this empirically through my observations of people and how their thoughts and behaviors reflect their philosophy of life. Often, my work entails reading between the lines to discover what is driving people in a particular direction.

Whatever your beliefs are, it's essential to be continually aware of this all-important part of our lives. The more your consciousness remains in a state of heightened spiritual awareness, the better off you will be as a human being. It's your key to transcending the trials of this life. The more aware you are, the better off. You can't help but be your higher self.

Of course, not everyone believes in a spiritual side of their lives, but nearly everyone is aware of something beyond their physical being.

America is having a rough time, but there's hope. This country has weathered many challenges, but things are different now. People need to carefully filter a high-speed, multichannel barrage of propaganda coming from all directions. Hopefully, we can effectively guide our thinking by using critical analytical skills, the observing ego, and good common sense. We all know that the deliberate manipulation of what passes as news contributes to the country's polarization. News outlets aren't the only ones to blame. Individuals themselves exert power over others through posts and other means. Govern yourself accordingly.

Remind yourself that there is no average American. We are a mixture of all cultures, races, and spiritual belief systems, including some people who choose not to believe in anything at all. There has always been room for all of this. That's the magic and promise of America.

A RETURN TO
FAITH AND VALUES

A close look at the cover of this book reveals what's troubling America's collective mind. The symptoms of our present mental state are concerning and far-reaching. I hope you've sensed while reading this book what it will take to put that mind back together again. We covered common sense earlier, and a good dose of that will go a long way toward healing this country.

Two other healing factors are found in the form of faith and values. Many of the issues facing the United States are the result of a fragmented value system that has lost touch with the basic principles that unify Americans rather than divide them.

It all starts with the home. Ideally, individuals are raised in families where traditions and learning right from wrong become imbedded in a child's psyche for future reference throughout life. Communities, schools, and religious institutions reinforce those values when consideration of others is their guiding philosophy. With children faith and values find fertile soil to create the foundation of a life that emphasizes civilized living within a social fabric. Respect for oneself and others can only be found in a value system that is based on kindness.

Unfortunately, a multitude of children are raised in single-parent or blended-family homes. Although such homes are capable of teaching faith and values and can certainly give children the right parental guidance, the truth is that those household scenarios are in general much more challenging and stressful. Another family issue is distraction.

Technology has enormous power to compete with parenting, and time spent learning offline is limited if not counteracted by the strong lure of the internet. Certainly, adults of all ages too have their faces perpetually in their screens. It's as though an invisible tractor beam is continually pulling them back to their devices. We've seen that values found online are often in direct opposition to what parents are trying to impart. Emphases on violence, material wealth, appearance, and derogatory language are found in abundance, especially in video games and social media.

Males are drawn heavily to gaming while females are all about social media platforms that emphasize beauty and lifestyles that are predominantly unattainable.

Another issue that needs our attention is that we are presently living in a society that increasingly finds our educational system on all levels imposing policies and curriculum that overstep parental rights to teach their own children. Inclusion is perfectly fine, but we are witnessing an age of overcompensation. *Overcompensation* occurs when excessive measures are taken to correct a perceived or real error, weakness, or problem. The danger in doing so is that it can readily backfire as common sense will perceive it as an exaggerated reaction.

When I served in the army, I was impressed with how promotion was based on a meritocracy. Moving up the ranks was based on time in grade (TIG) as well as demonstrated competence. A *meritocracy* is a system in which people are promoted in their field of endeavor based exclusively on their demonstrated ability and merit. Every effort should be made to provide opportunities to guarantee an equal playing field for everyone. Beyond that, rewards should be based on achievement.

Using proper manners and being polite toward others are cornerstone values that can go a very long way in making America sane again. In fact, manners are far more important than any legislation; manners reflect a respect and gratitude toward others that undermine confrontation or conflict. I always teach my clients that, while not foolproof, the more kindness and self-control you demonstrate in the face of conflict, the more you can control the outcome—not always, of course, but enough to warrant considering kindness and self-control as a strategy.

Faith refers to the complete trust and confidence that we can place in an individual or any other entity. On a spiritual level, it is often belief in the absence of proof. Trust can only be established by a conviction that you can release any doubt as to the truth of what you are being told.

Having a solid foundation of faith and a deeply rooted set of values can go a long way in supporting mental well-being. Without faith and values, a person has little to fall back on when coping with life's inevitable struggles.

From extensive experience, I know that people with a strong conviction in their faith fare better than those who have little belief or none at all. A solid foundation can resist any and all stresses.

One of America's most amazing gifts is the fact that people are free to believe in whatever way they wish. If faith and values are thoroughly imbued with a caring philosophy, then America's collective psyche will find its way during these challenging times. That can only happen through educating our children properly and cultivating tolerance.

MAKING AMERICA SANE AGAIN

Throughout this book, you've been exposed to a theme of personal responsibility, and that's for a simple reason. Rather than giving license to assume a feeling of helplessness, I'm encouraging empowerment. If you focus on a belief that you're powerless, then the conditions of depression and anxiety can flourish.

The insights I've offered and suggestions I've made represent micro changes that—taken together—can redirect the trajectory of the nation. Realistically, you can only control what is within your own life and sphere of influence. But everyone working even individually toward a common goal necessarily will have an accumulating effect.

For true sweeping changes to be made, we need to look at the macro changes that must occur. I'm careful not to take political sides here but instead base my suggestions on sound psychological principles. In this highly sensitized environment, it's easy to offend unintentionally.

So—what can America do on a national level to address some of our most pressing problems? Since I live in the real world, I recognize that these ideas are long shots, but here we go anyway.

Front and center is the national crisis of addiction. The pain and suffering that individuals and families go through when they've lost a loved one through drug overdoses—intentional and accidental—are tragic and often preventable. Helping to gain control over this truly far-reaching epidemic requires a strong and aggressive approach, something that pulls all sides together with a common goal that no one, apart from drug dealers, will contest. Once again, robust psychological evidence confirms common sense in that conflicting groups can work effectively together when they identify a mutually, highly defined goal.

So how do we address addiction? We need to implement a system that strongly emphasizes a model of personal responsibility that incentivizes healthy behaviors. And just how do we do that?

Here's where social comparison theory can help us. According to that model, individuals determine their own social and personal worth by self-assessing how they compare to others. We tend to measure ourselves according to whatever metrics matter to us.

If you doubt the power of social comparison, simply look at adolescents highly influenced by their peer group. Individuals who declare, "I don't care what other people think of me," are fooling no one, including themselves.

The primary educational system can be a great starting point for fighting addiction. Children need to be exposed early and often to a powerful series of messages that encourage healthy choices while rejecting poor ones. Parents need to be looped in, and we need not burden teachers with more responsibilities than they already have. Patterns established in childhood are resistant to change. Obese children become obese adults in most cases, especially if parents are similarly inclined.

We can enlist another resource I share in just a bit that's actually America's secret weapon.

Besides food addiction, we are beset by drug addiction of all types. Legal and illegal substances are destroying the fabric of America. This isn't hyperbole. It's fact.

As mentioned earlier, I see how lives are destroyed through unchecked addictions in my own practice. Families forever carry the burden of sadness and guilt over a loved one's overdose.

We'll take just the single but massive issue of fentanyl addiction. I could choose another drug of choice, but this example serves our purpose. As you probably already know, this synthetic opioid is much more addictive than heroin. Withdrawal is very painful, and once the hook is in, a person descends into a cycle of poverty, homelessness, and craving in which the only goal is the next fix to relieve the discomfort.

If you witnessed just one session in my office where a family is working through their loss of a loved one from overdose, you would understand the import of my words. Perhaps you or someone you know has felt the direct impact of one of these tragedies. Active addictions also take their toll on family and friends.

In my view, here's what we can do to help those in need. We place criminals in prison primarily for three reasons: keeping society safe, punishment, and hopefully a level of rehabilitation.

Addicts should not be viewed as criminals, though their dealers should. I hesitate to say they have a disease in the traditional sense, as we must be careful not to reject the idea of personal responsibility. Instead,

I work on a hybrid model that views addiction as a combination of psychological and physiological factors. The disease model comes into play when we recognize that addicted people suffer from a compulsive cycle of use that has biochemically seized their brains. People are responsible for the behavior that leads to addiction, but the receptor sites in their brains have a powerful vote in the matter. Certainly, environmental issues and genetic proclivities also play their part.

Just as we protect society from individuals whom we deem dangerous, we should also protect those who are a danger to themselves. Involuntary commitments to treatment facilities should be mandatory nationwide if a person is identified as severely drug addicted. Those criteria are easily established enough. A minimum of six months of treatment should be automatically mandated with up to a year, depending on the individual's progress. An addicted brain needs approximately ninety days to withdraw from the effects of the drug. A gradual reemergence of proper decision making and analytic functioning begins at that point.

If my suggestions seem too harsh, remember that one hundred thousand deaths annually from fentanyl add up one million lives lost in just ten years. That's if current death rates stabilize and don't increase, which is unlikely. Those numbers don't convey the depth of suffering that each death reflects. Families I've worked with would gladly support such a policy.

These tragedies are preventable. The freedom to abuse oneself should be forfeited in these special cases. Homelessness is completely preventable as well. While not making participation in such programs mandatory, we do have the resources to address this serious social problem. Providing a safe and clean living environment in exchange for a requirement that the homeless person follow certain rules should be available to all who need the help.

So how do we accomplish this lofty goal? For starters, the government wastes an enormous amount of money. I'm sure you would agree with that. Where we realign the budget is beyond the scope of this book.

What I can tell you is that we have a secret untapped resource available to us. **That secret weapon is human capital in the form of America's youth.**

America should expect all young adults somewhere in the range of eighteen to twenty-two years of age to perform a year of national service. We already have a suitable government agency in place through AmeriCorps. This major expansion in human resources would be a massive win-win for this nation.

It would provide us with enormous potential staffing for various programs.

It should provide benefits but low pay. The reason has to do with rewards. If I'm doing something of value for someone else and I'm rewarded excessively for it, that consideration can readily devalue the act itself. Think of it as an opportunity to do something selfless and build character.

Let's return to the addiction issue. We can repurpose into treatment centers facilities that are preferably away from urban areas. Nature plays a prominent role in healing. Those treatment centers would do their utmost to be self-sufficient as possible through farming initiatives. Growing as much food as possible will have a considerable impact on the collective experience of the residents. You get the idea. The agency can staff the centers primarily with young adults who have received basic training targeting their responsibilities.

Not only would we benefit from the energy and optimism of youth, but young adults would experience something that they would value for the rest of their lives. Think of the camaraderie when evolving, cohesive teams share a common set of goals. I'm well aware that scores of disheartened youths have lost a sense of hope and optimism, but that can be changed by establishing an expectation of service to the country and their fellow human beings.

Think about the impact of teachers having more aides to help them in the classroom or older citizens in nursing homes having someone assigned to them to visit regularly. This type of activity is apparent now as many Americans already volunteer, but we need to scale it up. Remember Cicero (and JFK): "Ask what you can do for your country."

While I'm on a roll here, I believe we should establish a new agency titled the Department of Ethical Conduct and Conflict Resolution primarily targeting internal use.

The government itself needs to act in a much more mature way. Additionally, just as we have public health warnings on tobacco and alcohol products, public service announcements associated with excess news exposure would be a promising idea. I can dream, can't I?

Our educational system should place a heavy emphasis on teaching children critical life skills. These skills should include lessons in how to be physically and psychologically healthy human beings who care for others. A colleague of mine, Dr. Michelle Sukenik, has developed an excellent video series that reflects this initiative titled *Mindful Minutes*. As the name suggests, these videos each run for a minute and cover a wide range of topics essential to a child's emotional growth. You can find these on her YouTube channel. Many of these values and skills are learned at home, but realistically, many are not.

What children are taught at home and at school creates a value system that reflects the best of those principles upon which America was founded. These core American values include individual freedoms, respect for others, equal opportunity, humanitarianism, faith, and democracy. The responsibility for the values children learn, or fail to learn, begins at home.

Common sense, faith, and values will help to restore America to a healthier psychological state. It's not that hard to understand that these times have created a divide among people that media sources of all kinds constantly reinforce to enhance their bottom lines.

Only you as an individual can become an enlightened consumer of information. Tolerance and understanding are powerful tools that can bring us closer together.

I once interviewed an individual on my radio show who had been happily married for fifty-plus years. I asked him the clichéd question as to the secret of their success.

"That's easy," he said. "We follow the 51 percent rule."

He saw that I was a bit confused and quickly added, "I give 51 percent and so does my wife."

I understood immediately. My hope is that we can all go even further than that in all our relationships.

I'd like to share one final thought about where you fit into all of this as an individual with respect to how you can help.

At times, I like to use analogies to explain a complex concept to a client or a class I'm teaching. Here, use your inventive mind for a moment or two. Imagine that each of us is a cell in a massive, complex human body that we call America. That body is experiencing significant and even life-threatening inflammation in multiple areas. Say you had a choice. What if you could choose that your individual cell would function as one that contributes to inflammation by agitating the other cells within your reach? All you would need to do is repeat negative messaging and fear to any cell you can touch. Since fear is highly contagious, your impact will only be limited by your amplitude and range of influence.

On the other hand, you could instead choose to be a T cell that protects the body by meeting any threat with an immune response. That response comes in the form of kindness and other behaviors that promote healing. Faith and values are also powerful antibodies.

Fellow T cells will immediately recognize you and join in on any positive response. While negativity begets negativity, the converse is also true. Positive energy engenders a synergistic response in others who share the same orientation. Optimists are simply realists who expect challenges in life and then overcome them by filtering through the negative to embrace the positive.

The choice of what role you want to play is entirely up to you. Now that you hopefully understand what forces are in play that influence your attitudes and behavior, you can awaken from the mass hypnosis that has subtlety created a backdrop of life in America that is dominated by pessimism. Hypnosis is achieved through either overload of the central nervous system or by causing it to be fatigued. Either condition sets the stage for *trance induction*, a state of heightened suggestibility in which critical mental faculties are reduced and the mind is more open to suggestions.

When the human mind is susceptible to influences, then repeated, unrelenting messages that might otherwise be rejected are now more easily incorporated.

Whether intentionally created or not, propaganda is a great hypnotist.

I listen very carefully as part of my profession, and I hear evidence of this hypnosis on a regular basis. When someone speaks in sound bites that quite obviously aren't their own, I wonder if they've synthesized what they've heard, seen, or read. "Drinking the Kool-Aid" and "Wake up and smell the coffee" have become part of our national mainstream lexicon.

We need to keep in mind that America is a country with a strong history of individuals representing divergent backgrounds who pull together to meet a common challenge. In the simplest of terms, the major challenge facing this country is not succumbing to the negative forces that are in play that are keeping us divided as a people.

If the disease can be identified as being a negative mindset, then you the reader are most certainly the cure.

A PERSONAL NOTE

What follows is my personal set of beliefs. These beliefs work well for me, and I hope that yours work well for you. As a Christian, my direction in life is clear. For me, the teachings of Jesus Christ have laid out a path that makes perfect sense in a fallen world. I begin each day with a reading from *Jesus Calling* by Sarah Young. It provides me with thoughts to reflect on throughout the day. The readings are inspiring, and most importantly, they remind me to stay in the moment and appreciate God's love for us. The messages are at once simple and profound.

A Christian life is a challenging one in which the goal is to live as closely as possible in accord with the teachings of Christ. I view Christ as the human incarnation of God on earth who arrived from another dimension. I believe that life here is a training ground, and for those who pass, we are given the opportunity to graduate and move on to that other dimension.

In my practice, it's essential to be able to pivot every hour from one set of complex dynamics and issues to the next without being distracted. My solution is a simple one. I briefly say a prayer that I will be guided in my work to help the next client in their struggles. It helps that I have great fondness for them.

I do believe that God choreographs for good and explored this concept in one of my earlier books, *God's Shrink*. I experience acts of intervention on a regular basis. It comes in various forms, but for our purposes, I'll mention appointments made and cancelled.

I often receive calls from clients I haven't seen in a long time. The interesting part is that they will have shown up in either a dream or passed through my mind the day *before* they contact me. On other occasions, I may get an appointment cancellation, and then someone urgently in need of a session contacts me shortly thereafter so I'm able to see them. These events and others happen at a rate that defies coincidence. Perhaps you have had similar experiences. I genuinely believe our paths in life contain many of these experiences if we are open to receiving them.

Of course, people take many other spiritual paths. If you follow a particular faith, consider it a blueprint. I like to say that various forms of faith are like different tribes on the same reservation. Celebrating the similarities, in my view, is more important than looking at the differences. Certainly, a spiritually based philosophy can be informally lived as well.

As of this writing, the pandemic continues to create fear in an already anxious world. The war in Ukraine dominates contemporary headlines.

Fears about both situations have affected people in diverse ways. In my experience, the worry about the pandemic has been worse than the pandemic itself. It has caused a massive amount of social, educational, physical, and emotional distress that will be impossible to quantify accurately. Once an alarm is sounded and just keeps going off without restraint, it produces nothing more than excess stress. I trust we all intuitively understand that.

This, too, shall pass.

There will always be a new crisis to take hold in the minds of those who are vulnerable to worry. Anxiety moves easily from one concern to the next. Learning to manage stress by putting it in perspective is the key to living a balanced life. Stress is a part of life but doesn't need to be its focus.

And now for the inescapable truth:

Each of us will pass away. It's inevitable. It's also a subject that makes many people uncomfortable. We have an intellectual awareness that we will die, but we mostly live in a state of denial on a psychological level. Not me, not today.

Full awareness of our mortality creates a unique opportunity to consider what is profoundly important. So, from this very moment forward, as you read this sentence, ask yourself this one question: *In the time I have left in this life, what kind of person do I want to be?* Spend time contemplating your answer. It's the most important question you can ask yourself. Maybe you believe you're fully on track, or perhaps you need to make some minor or major adjustments. In any case, my wish for you is that your life is filled with love and a deep sense of purpose. Try and leave the world a better place because of your presence in it.

Make America sane again by being better citizens and residents, by spreading positive energy at every opportunity. Any act of kindness, tolerance, and understanding has profound effects. Your sphere of influence reaches much further than you can imagine.

May God bless you on your journey.

AN INVITATION

It gives me great pleasure to hear from readers. Please visit my website at:

makeamericasaneagain.net

ABOUT THE AUTHOR

Michael Adamse received his Ph.D. in Clinical Psychology from the University of Miami after completing a pre-doctoral fellowship at Yale University. He was appointed as an Adjunct Assistant Professor at both the University of Miami and Nova Southeastern University, where he lectured worldwide. He also served as a Captain in the Medical Corps, U.S. Army Reserve.

Dr. Adamse specializes in relationship issues and has practiced for over forty years. He is an expert psychological commentator on many issues and has participated in over 300 radio, print, and TV interviews.

His first book, *Affairs of the Net*, published by HCI Books in 1996, represented a cutting-edge online relationship study. In addition, Dr. Adamse has appeared on multiple national media outlets in recognition of his expertise in this area.

Dr. Adamse's first novel, *Anniversary*, published in 1998, is an inspirational story and represents HCI Books' first fiction-based book in over twenty-five years of publishing. The book was translated and released in Japan, Poland, and Hungary.

His novel, *God's Shrink*, was published by HCI Books in 2007 and was met with critical acclaim. The book was translated and released in Japan, where it achieved best-seller status. It was also released in Poland, Portugal, and Brazil. In addition, he co-authored the screenplay, which is in development.

Dr. Adamse also hosted a weekly National Public Radio Show, *On the Couch*, which featured interviews with various nationally recognized leaders in literature, the arts, entertainment, politics, and the media.

Made in the USA
Columbia, SC
06 July 2022

62676641R00080